GW00482726

THATCHAM URC200

~ 1804 - 2004 ~

HISTORY OF THE INDEPENDENT CHAPEL
OF THATCHAM

LATER KNOWN AS THE
CONGREGATIONAL CHAPEL (CHURCH)

AND LATER STILL AS THE
UNITED REFORMED CHURCH

Roy Brian Tubb

Front cover: British School and United Reformed Church,1992.
The girls by the doorway were members of Mrs Robinson's ballet class.

Back cover: Church Lane about 1900.

Published for the
United Reformed Church, Thatcham
by
Henwick Worthy Books
13 Elmhurst Road
Thatcham, Berkshire
RG18 3DQ
Tel: (01635) 867-105

from where copies of this book may be obtained.

Printed by The Alpha Xperience
148 Kings Road
Newbury, Berkshire

CONTENTS

DEDICATION

This
book is
dedicated to
all those people
who have contributed in
some measure, large or small,
to the life of our church over the past
two hundred years. Their Christian witness
over that period has enabled the church
to prosper in good times and endure
in difficult times. It is thanks to
them that this little piece
of history could be
written.

FOREWORD BY THE MINISTER

In December 2004 we at Thatcham URC celebrated the church's 200th anniversary. An anniversary is a wonderful event. It is a time of preparation, a time of gathering, an occasion for the church family to be revitalized. It is a time of looking back and looking forward. It is a time to draw breath and stand before the stories, memories and pictures. It is a time to stand before the mystery of everything that we are as individuals, a mystery that began long before human memory, when God's love first spilled over in creation, a mystery that will extend far beyond our lives on this Earth.

Coming to Thatcham URC in September 2001, I caught the vision of this church to serve the wider community of Thatcham – spiritually through worship and physically through a wide range of ancillary buildings. The completion this year of the first phase of the refurbishment of the buildings has taken us one step forward to meet that vision. It is a vision founded in two hundred years of service to the people of Thatcham, a vision that we, as a church, continue to explore creatively as we endeavour to make the love of Christ known through our words and our actions in a world struggling with pain and disappointment, conflict and injustice.

Revd Barbara Flood-Page

PASTORS AND MINISTERS OF THE CHURCH

Various Students from different theological colleges: 1804-1805
Mr WALKER: end of 1805 - Nov 1806
Mr ISAAC: 1807-09
Supply Preachers: 1809-10
Revd William ASH: 1810-17
Mr Peter SIBREE: 1817-18
Revd Ralph WARDLE: 1818-41
Revd Marcus HOPWOOD: 1843-49
Revd Ebenezer WHITE: 1849-59
Revd Charles GOWAR: 1861-72
Revd William Mills ROBINSON: 1873-80
Revd Edwin Jenkin GRIFFITHS: 1881-99
Revd Jasper J FREWING: 1900-06
Revd Jesse George DAVIS: 1907-17
Revd John STAY: 1918-33
Revd Arthur Enford RICHMOND: 1933-42
Revd Owen Evan OWEN: 1943-50
Revd Roy BOOTH: 1951-62
Revd Frederick SPRIGGS: 1962-73
Revd Arthur BAKER: 1974-89
Revd Daphne Celia WILLIAMS: 1989-93
Revd Nina MEAD: 1994-98
Revd Barbara Jane FLOOD-PAGE: 2001-

INTRODUCTION

It is my privilege to present this account of the first 200 years of the history of this church. Considerably longer and much more detailed than earlier histories of the church, this book should provide easy access to many past events that are far from easy to unravel from official records. Included within the following pages are several extracts from the official minutes of church meetings. Such minutes are not always as clear or informative as one might wish but the language itself often presents a fascinating insight into the atmosphere of a bygone age.

Many events recorded here may seem to have been quite routine and of little concern to the 'big picture', while some will clearly strike one as having been of considerable signifiance. All events taken together should portray a balanced perspective. There are omissions - it would be impossible to complete such a work without them. I believe, however, that I have captured snippets of most of the happenings over the past 200 years. It is hoped that this book will provide an interesting record of the history of the church, which began its life in 1804 as the Independent Chapel in Church Lane, Thatcham.

Finally, may I thank all those persons (mostly members or former members of the church) who have assisted me by providing useful information. Grateful thanks are also hereby given to staff in Newbury Library, Newbury Museum and the Berkshire County Record Office, Reading.

R B Tubb, August 2005

BOOKS BY THE SAME AUTHOR

Thatcham Road Names
Cold Ash & Ashmore Green: Road by Road
Through the Eyes of a Clerk
Speen, Stockcross & Shaw-cum-Donnington: Road by Road
Greenham: Road by Road

The Church (1905).
This picture appeared in Revd Summers' booklet to mark the centenary of
Thatcham Congregational Church.

URC200
(1804-2004)

**HISTORY OF THE INDEPENDENT CHAPEL OF THATCHAM,
LATER KNOWN AS THE CONGREGATIONAL CHAPEL
OR CHURCH AND LATER STILL AS THE
UNITED REFORMED CHURCH**

THE BEGINNING OF NONCONFORMITY

Although the year 1804 saw the building of the Independent Chapel in Church Lane, Thatcham, it did not herald the beginning of Nonconformity - neither in this country at large, nor in Thatcham. A brief review of its origins may help to clarify the importance of the building of our church.

One significant date in the development of Nonconformity is that of 1378, when John Wycliffe (a philosopher-theologian) was summoned to a Church Court at Lambeth and accused of heresy against the Church of Rome. Wycliffe had denied the doctrine of transubstantiation - the sacramental doctrine which maintained that the wine was changed to the blood of Christ and the bread to the flesh of his body. He also stressed the importance of preaching (in preference to liturgy) and the primacy of the Bible, to which everybody should, he said, have access in their own language. Wycliffe was never actually put on trial but in 1380 he was forced out of Oxford University. He died in 1384. Followers of Wycliffe, who became known derogatively as Lollards (mumblers), were responsible for a translation of the Bible into English. They grew in number until repression was ordered by Henry IV. The Lollards' first martyr was William Sawtrey, who was burned at the stake in 1401. The movement went underground until about 1500, when a revival began.

Soon after that time, the Anabaptists came to prominence. They repudiated infant baptism, holding the belief that infants were not responsible for sin because they were too young to have any awareness of good and evil. The Anabaptist movement originated in Zurich, Switzerland. Its first adult baptism took place near Zurich in 1525. By then, Martin Luther had made his impact in Germany - he had proclaimed the Bible to be the only and supreme authority on questions of religious faith, not pope, nor cardinals, nor bishops. Believers, he said, were justified by faith in Christ, not by works or penances: they needed no priest to give them pardon or absolution. The anti-papal sentiment in England was fuelled in Henry VIII's reign by the annulment in 1533 of his marriage to Catherine of Aragon and Henry's resultant excommunication from Rome.

In 1558 Queen Mary I died and her sister Elizabeth became Queen of England. By the Act of Supremacy 1559, Queen Elizabeth became the Supreme Governor of the Church in all matters temporal and spiritual. This Act effectively established the Church of England. Also in 1559 the Act of Uniformity outlawed the celebration of mass by Roman Catholics and the administration of holy communion, baptism and the conducting of worship by Presbyterian ministers. Baptism of adults by Anabaptists was also made a crime. The effect of the Act was to stoke the fire of Nonconformity.

In the 17th century, there were many in the Church of England who believed that the Church needed purifying of its 'popish' ritualism and idolatry - they emphasized plain preaching and the intensity of religious experience as derived from a covenant relationship with God. During a controversy over vestments in the 1560s, these Dissenters became known as Puritans. Some tried to reform the Church of England from within - they urged Parliament to set up a presbyterian administration (eldership) for the Church. Other Puritans, discouraged by the long delay in reform, decided to separate themselves from the Church of England. These became known as Separatists and eventually evolved into Presbyterians, Baptists, Independents (Congregationalists), Quakers or one of several smaller more radical groups, such as Levellers, Diggers and Fifth Monarchy Men.

One early Separatist leader was Robert Browne, who established an Independent Church at Norwich in 1580. As a consequence of his activities he was imprisoned thirty-two times until in 1582 he was exiled. Browne subsequently returned to England and conformed to the Established Church. From 1583, when John Whitgift became Archbishop of Canterbury, the persecution of Nonconformists was fierce. The largest congregations were probably those in prisons, where many were never called to trial: some were cast in irons and some died from hunger or illness while serving their sentences. All were daily defamed, being accused of sedition and heresy.

In 1593 drastic legislation was introduced, whereby those who refused to attend their parish churches and attended Nonconformist meetings instead, were liable to have their goods and lands confiscated and could even be ordered to leave the country. Failure to obey the order rendered them liable to execution. Separatists John Greenwood and Henry Barrow were hanged on 6th April 1593. Separatist John Penry was hanged on 29th May that same year. It was soon after this time that many Separatists emigrated to North America. The Pilgrim Fathers of New England sailed into Plymouth, Massachusetts, in 1620.

The English Civil War of 1642-51, which also involved the Scots, was intricately bound up with religion. Parliament's sympathy lay with the Separatists. Oliver Cromwell himself was a Separatist - an Independent. Most of the Separatist groups enjoyed freedom of worship from 1651 until the Restoration of the Monarchy in 1660, when Charles II became King. His

Parliament passed an Act of Uniformity in 1662 - this required all preachers to swear an oath of canonical obedience and all churches to use the Book of Common Prayer. It was not until 1689, during the reign of William and Mary, that the Toleration Act was passed - this provided religious freedom for the Separatists but maintained restrictions on Roman Catholics and Unitarians. By 1709 the three main dissenting denominations (Presbyterian, Baptist and Independent-Congregational) had built about 1,000 meeting-houses.

The religious zeal of the late 17th century subsequently declined and rationalism became more popular but eventually an evangelical revival occurred. This resulted in the Missionary Movement and the founding of Sunday Schools and Weekday Schools. New preachers proclaimed the gospel with passionate intensity. In 1738 John Wesley and George Whitefield began a Methodist Revival from within the Church of England. The Methodist Society did not originally intend to break with the Church of England - the break came in 1795, four years after John Wesley's death. The Revivalists, which included the Independent Churches, called people to repentance and to a new life of virtue, responsibility and service. This led to various charitable and educational societies being formed. The London Missionary Society was founded in 1795. The National School Society (Anglican) was founded in 1811 - it was fostered by the Society for the Promotion of Christian Knowledge, which itself was founded in 1699. The British and Foreign School Society (Nonconformist) was founded in 1814.

Independent Churches or Chapels were governed by their own congregations but as part of the plan to spread the gospel, county associations were formed. The word 'Congregational' was eventually adopted by most Independent Chapels but there does not appear to have been a precise date for this change. The Congregational Magazine was founded in 1818. The Congregational Union of England and Wales was formed in 1832. However, the description 'Independent Chapel' remained in use for many years. Although the description 'Congregational Church' occurs in the Thatcham Independent Chapel's minute book from 1850 onward, the description 'Independent Chapel' also occurs until 1873, when its use appears to have ceased.

On 5th October 1972 the Congregational Church in England and Wales united with the Presbyterian Church of England to form the United Reformed Church. A relatively small number of Congregational Churches did not join the union. On 21st September 1981 the Church of Christ (the small British counterpart of the American Disciples of Christ) joined the United Reformed Church and on 1st April 2000 the Congregational Union of Scotland joined.

THE BEGINNING IN THATCHAM

Perhaps the earliest recorded Dissenter in Thatcham was Nicholas Fuller (barrister). He became Lord of the Manor of Chamberhouse, when his purchase of the estate was completed in 1585. Mr Fuller, after whom Fuller Close in Thatcham is named, took an active interest in the affairs of Thatcham Parish. His zeal for justice and his strong desire to defend the cause of the poor led to improvements in the administration of local charities and better benefits for the poor. The Puritan tendencies of Mr Fuller led him to become a champion of the Nonconformists. This in turn led to his imprisonment in 1607. As a barrister, he defended Thomas Ladd for attending a Nonconformist meeting and Richard Maunsell for being a Puritan preacher. Both defendants had been charged by the Ecclesiastical Commissioners and Mr Fuller argued that the Commissioners had no authority either to imprison or to fine his clients. King James I, however, sided with Archbishop Bancroft, who fined the barrister £200 and imprisoned him for nearly four months, probably in the Lollards Tower at Lambeth Palace.

A noteworthy event occurred in Thatcham in 1662, the year of the Uniformity Act in the reign of King Charles II. The Vicar of Thatcham at that time was Thomas Voisey and he was one of 2,000 Church of England clergymen who were evicted from their livings throughout the land. The following note was written in our church minute book by Revd W Mills Robinson on 17th April 1879 - "The Revd Thomas Voysey (or Voisey) was Vicar of this Parish and being a Puritan was ejected by the infamous Act of Uniformity. He returned to his native county Devonshire and resumed preaching but his excessive labours (at Plymouth) threw him into a fever of which he died in 1668."

We may reasonably suppose that Revd Voisey was far from being the only Puritan in Thatcham at that time. Indeed, so significant was that event of 24th August 1662 that 200 years later on 24th August 1862 the Congregational Chapel in Thatcham celebrated its bicentenary. The sermons preached on that Sunday were clearly related to the steadfast and practical faith of Thomas Voisey (see page 29).

In 1669 it was reported to the Bishop of Salisbury that in Thatcham, with a population of 865, there were just eighteen Separatists. In truth there were probably several more of that persuasion, being fearful of admitting their allegiance. An indication of the stricture of the laws in those days may be gleaned from the fact that in 1671 Andrew Pike, a shoemaker in Thatcham, was reported to the Bishop and charged with being absent from Holy Communion for eighteen months. Later, in 1731, four persons in Thatcham were reported by Revd Spackman for shaving on the Sabbath Day and neglecting the public worship.

Revd Voisey did not go away quietly in 1662. It is believed that he was involved in a serious vestry disturbance at St Nicolas' Church in Newbury on 12th April 1664 (Tuesday after Easter Day). The Mayor and Corporation of Newbury had met to appoint churchwardens and sidesmen, when they were assaulted "in a most barbarous manner ... by a rude and confused multitude" as reported at the time. The protesters also "made an outcry and noyse in the church, as if they had been bear baiting" during a service.

It was also around that time that Revd Voisey was apprehended for a 'plot' in the north-country, after having been reported by a neighbouring gentleman, whom some time earlier the Vicar had reproved for dissolute living. Revd Voisey was charged, found guilty and committed to Reading Jail and later removed to Windsor Castle. After serving fifteen months in prison, Voisey was released on bail by an old college friend, Lord Clifford, who provided the £500 required.

Nonconformity in Thatcham therefore had its roots long before 1804. Just before that year, Archer Thompson became Vicar of Thatcham. Thomas Henry Brown of Thatcham (a member of Thatcham Congregational Church for fifty-four years) wrote that Revd Thompson "was so good a preacher that (in 1793) he was elected evening preacher in the chapel of Magdalen Hospital, London, where he attracted the highest in the land to the services but while he was in London the services in Thatcham were neglected". Consequently some parishioners looked elsewhere for their spiritual nourishment. By this time Independents at Crookham had in 1791 already established an Independent meeting-room in a private house and a Baptist meeting-house was set up at Crookham in 1799. In the village of Thatcham, Samson Higgs opened a room for independent worship in 1800. John Barfield is known to have been a sympathiser. In 1802 John Barfield attempted to purchase the right to appoint the Vicar of Thatcham but failed. In December of that same year John Berry of Newbury began a weekly series of prayer meetings in various private houses in Thatcham. He subsequently joined with John Barfield, who by August 1803 was holding such meetings in a house, owned by Mrs Hannah Baily and occupied by Mr Barfield at that time.

John Barfield then threw in his lot with the Independents and decided that a proper meeting-house should be built in Thatcham. He purchased bricks from *Dunston House*, which was then being demolished and with those bricks he had the Independent Chapel built in Church Lane. The first trust deed for the administration of the chapel was drawn up on 20th June 1804. The Bishop of Salisbury was informed by letter of 1st December that same year. The chapel was entered in the official register on 8th December. The first service in the chapel was almost certainly held on Tuesday, 18th December 1804. Another date (13th December), which was added in the church minute book several years later is probably incorrect.

In his last report as church secretary in 1923, Horatio Skillman quoted from the *Evangelical Magazine* of January 1805. He wrote "On December 18th, 1804 a new meeting place was opened at Thatcham near Newbury. The place was crowded and the preachers were Mr Elliott of Devizes in the morning and Mr Cooke of Maidenhead in the evening; the ministers who otherwise engaged were from Reading, Wallingford, Goring, Hungerford and Newbury. In this place the Gospel is to be preached to the poor and probably to the poor only."

THE FIRST SERVICE

There were, apparently, no minutes recorded from 1804 to 1811. The only local information we have on the opening service was recorded by Revd W Mills Robinson on 23rd July 1874. He wrote that "The Revd R Elliott of Devizes preached in the morning from Psalm 118, verse 25 'Save now etc'. The Revd John Cooke of Maidenhead preached in the evening from Isaiah 51, verses 1 & 2 - there was a large assembly - but so infuriated was Satan and some of the Rabble of the Parish that Mr Barfield was burnt in effigy and the attendants at the services pelted with stones and mud. This testimony was given me by Mrs Morton senior of Bucklebury and Mrs Harper of Tadley."

Opposition to the Independent Chapel continued for some time. John Adnams of Harts Hill Farm, who was about fifteen years of age in 1804, recalled at later date to his colleagues how in those early days, he was met on Sunday mornings by men playing "rough music" on pots and kettles. John remained loyal to the Independent Chapel and was eventually made a deacon of the church.

From its inception in 1804 Thatcham Independent Chapel was probably under the pastoral care of Revd John Winter of Newbury until March 1812. It was certainly under his care in November 1811 - a note to that effect is written in the church minute book. It seems that for the first few years various students from different theological colleges led the services. However, two preachers stayed for a considerable time - a Mr Walker preached here from the end of 1805 until November 1806 and a Mr Isaac from early in 1807 until June or July 1809. After another year of supply preachers, the first minister to be ordained in the Independent Chapel was appointed (see next page).

WE SOLEMNLY UNITE

Although reference has just been made to "a large assembly" at the first service in 1804, there does not appear to have been any formal membership until seven years later, when a statement of the members' belief and commitment was drafted. It was dated 12th November 1811 and read -

"We whose names are hereunder written, perceiving that great spiritual advantage is to be derived from a real and professed union and communion under Christ the great Head of the Church, Do in his name and expectation of his blessing and under his authority heartily and solemnly unite ourselves in church fellowship as a separate church of Jesus Christ yet desiring to maintain a sincere affection towards all other churches under the same great Head and maintaining the same faith which we consider to be built on the foundation of the Holy Scriptures."

This statement was signed by just five members, namely, Samson Higgs, Thomas Pocock, Ann Higgs, John Carter (his mark) and John Barfield.

TEN MEMBERS, THE FIRST COMMUNION

Just over six weeks later (27th December 1811) ten more persons expressed an interest in membership - they "proposed themselves to become members"

17

and another person wished to be transferred to Thatcham from Goring-on-Thames. One year later at a church meeting held on the morning of 9th December 1812, the following five persons were admitted as members: Ann Barfield, Jesse Mears, William Carter, William Pocock and James Rhoads. In the afternoon of that same day these five new members and other members of the church attended a divine service, at which the Lord's Supper was for the first time administered in the chapel.

TWENTY PIONEERS

So at the end of 1812 there were just ten signed-up members in our Independent Chapel. Eight years passed before this number was to double. In April 1820 the church roll comprised the following twenty members - Revd William Ash, Mrs Adams, James Andrews, Ann Barfield, John Barfield, William Carter, Thomas Cooper, Matthew Corker, Thomas Fassett, James Fisher, Mrs Giles, Mr Hemming, Mrs Hemming, Thomas Hope, Thomas Lane, Jesse Mears, Elizabeth Mundy, Master Pocock, Thomas Pocock and Richard Wells.

REVD WILLIAM ASH (1810-1817)

William Ash, who started preaching at the Thatcham Independent Chapel in June 1810, remained on probation here until March 1812 but it was not until 17th June 1813 that he was ordained in the chapel. The following ministers were present on that day - Revds Winter and Dryland of Newbury, Douglas of Reading, Sloper of Devizes, Jefferson of Basingstoke and Pinnell of Mortimer.

William was born in Wakefield, Yorkshire, in 1778. He attended a training college at Rotherham. Revd William Henry Summers (Congregational minister at Hungerford) wrote in 1905 that William Ash had been brought up in the Moravian Church - a Protestant Church founded in England by immigrants from Moravia (which would currently lie in the Czech Republic). He also mentioned that William Ash "held charge of a church at Southend for a short time before settling at Thatcham". The fact that William was ordained here, rather than inducted, suggests that the church at Southend was Moravian.

It is not known where William Ash resided in his early days in Thatcham but on 9th June 1815 he married Ann Druce, widow, who lived at Thatcham Farm. William then moved into the farmhouse, currently known as *The Grange* in Church Gate. The pair were married in St Mary's Parish Church, Thatcham. There has been some confusion over the date of William Ash's year of resignation (because of failing health) from his position as Independent minister. Samuel Barfield recorded it as July 1817. Barfield also stated that a Peter Sibree succeeded William Ash and stayed for several months before he left sometime during 1818 to further his studies. However, William Ash appears to have remained living in Thatcham for at least a couple of years after 1818. He was listed as a church member at the Thatcham Independent Chapel in 1820 (see previous page).

Writing shortly after the time that Barfield's work was published, Revd Summers recorded in 1905 that Revd Ash resigned in 1825 - the reason for believing that was the year of his resignation may have been because the next minister's name (Revd Wardle) was first mentioned in the church minute book in 1825. Nevertheless, Revd Wardle appears to have been living in Thatcham in 1820 and was probably here in 1818. In September 1820, one of his daughters (Mary) was baptized in the Thatcham Independent Chapel. Furthermore, a gravestone, which currently leans against the front (western) wall of the church, records the death of Ralph, infant son of Ralph and Hannah Wardle, in September 181X (the last digit X being indistinct but see pages 20 and 21). All these factors taken together suggest that Samuel Barfield's account is correct and that the changeover of ministers occurred during 1817-18. It is worth recording here that the date of Revd Ash's resignation as stated in the 150th anniversary booklet is merely a repeat of that given by Revd Summers in 1905, namely 1825.

Revd Summers added that William Ash eventually "went into business, though still preaching on Sundays near his new home in Hampshire". Sometime after resigning his post here, William Ash moved northward and continued his ministry, firstly at Loughborough and then at Doncaster. The census taken in April 1851 recorded that William and his wife Ann were then living in Doncaster. William's age was given as seventy-two and Ann's as seventy. William died at Spring Gardens, Doncaster on 19th October 1851, aged seventy-three. William and Ann had at least one child, a daughter named Ann Druce Ash, who was baptized at the Independent Chapel, Thatcham, on 13th January 1817.

Collections in the early days of our church were made only at the monthly communion service. Total collection for the period February 1812 to April 1813 was £3-13-0, while the total of disbursements for the same period was £2-0-6, leaving a surplus of £1-12-6 carried forward.

REVD RALPH WARDLE (1818-1841)

Ralph Wardle was baptized as Ralph Wardale on 3rd August 1783, the son of William and Isabel Wardale, at Bywell, Northumberland. As mentioned earlier, the first mention of this minister in the church minute book occurred in 1825 on January 2nd, when he was given £1 to distribute to those in need. Also mentioned earlier is the fact one of his children was baptized in our church in 1820, so Ralph and Hannah Wardle appear to have moved to Thatcham by 1820. Prior to that year two older children of theirs were baptized elsewhere, namely William at Banbury (Oxfordshire) on 7th December 1813 and Richard at Wednesbury (Staffordshire) on 26th August 1816. Five children of Ralph and Hannah were baptized in our church - Mary on 24th September 1820, John on 18th September 1822, James on 12th April 1825, Isabella on 31st December 1826 and Elizabeth on 31st March 1829.

At the time of writing (2005), there are two gravestones that remain leaning against the western wall of the church. One of these was referred to on page

19: it relates to three children of Ralph and Hannah Wardle. The first child mentioned is Ralph, who died aged three months on 5th September and although the year is not absolutely clear, it is almost certainly 1818. Young Ralph does not appear to have been baptized. The two other children mentioned are Elizabeth, who died 9th July 1832 aged three years eight months and Isabella, who died two days later on 11th July 1832 aged five years seven months.

In the summer of 1824 John Barfield purchased a plot of land in Park Lane and had a house built there. It was completed the following year at Mr Barfield's expense. He gave it to the trustees of the Independent Chapel by transfer deed dated 28th May 1825. It was to be used as a residence for the minister of the chapel, so presumably Revd Wardle and his family lived there from 1825. The house, which is still there, currently has the name *The Old Manse* and is numbered as 24 Park Lane.

Although Revd Wardle was pastor of the chapel for about twenty-three years, little is known about his time here: the only minutes that were written during that period consist of a record of the monthly sacramental collections and the disbursements, which apart from the purchase of communion wine, consisted of payments to those in need. The collections averaged £5-14-6 (£5·725) per year from 1820 until 1833: records then ceased until 1841. The absence of any records during those eight years may signify that Revd Wardle was not in good health and that a prolonged period of inactivity ensued. Whatever the reason, in August 1841 the first deacons were elected (see next page). This action was probably carried out by members to get the chapel back into proper administrative and spiritual order. It seems most likely that Revd Wardle had just resigned at that time. He was then fifty-eight years of age. In 1851 Ralph and Hannah were living in Broad Street (Thatcham Broadway). Ralph was described in the census of that year as a "pauper, formerly an Independent minister".

Ralph Wardle was the author of theological works on *Regeneration*, *Justification* and *The Dealings of God with Adam*. He died in 1854 and was buried, apparently under the lawn at the front of the Independent Chapel, on 8th March 1854, nearly seventy-one years of age.

THE FIRST DEACONS - JOHN BARFIELD & JOHN DRINKWATER

At 7 o'clock in the evening on 11th August 1841, a church meeting was held in the vestry. It was convened for the purpose of choosing deacons: Mr John Barfield and Mr John Drinkwater were elected by the members assembled, all of whom 'signed' the church minute book. In fact only three actually signed - John Adnams (witness), John Barfield and John Drinkwater. The other six made their marks - John Carter, James Child, Joseph Clarage, George Emmans, Thomas Giles and Richard Tull. This appointment of deacons appears to have been prompted by a serious illness of Revd Wardle and his eventual resignation.

REVD MARCUS HOPWOOD (1843-1849)

The only known detailed reference to the ministry of Marcus Hopwood is that which described the occasion of his departure from Thatcham. It was probably his successor, Ebenezer White, who recorded that "The Revd Marcus Hopwood resigned the Pastorate of this Christian Church in April 1849. A public meeting was held in the Chapel, Tuesday April 3rd, 1849. Revd Robert Hinslie of London in the chair. Mr Edward Hunt, deacon*, presented a silver inkstand in the name of 120 subscribers as a testimonial of the respect and appreciation in which Mr Hopwood had been held during the six years of his ministry. Pleasing testimony was also borne to the kindness and works of charity of his beloved wife. The Revd Spedding Curwen of Reading took part in the interesting service."

*Mr Hunt did not become a deacon until October 1851, so this statement must have been written after that time.

According to Samuel Barfield, Marcus Hopwood "came from the Dissenting College at Exeter". The first mention of Revd Hopwood's name in the minute book may be that of 4th November 1843, when an indeterminate 'Hopwood' was given 2/6 (12½ pence). Revd Hopwood first administered the sacrament of holy communion at the Independent Chapel, Thatcham, on 5th May 1844. The name of the pastor's wife was probably Matilda Hopwood, who was listed as being one of the "members admitted into church fellowship during the pastorate of the Revd M Hopwood" at Thatcham.

There was no organ in the church at this time. It was recorded later that by 1844 Edmund Pinnock (senior) was playing a violin in church to accompany the hymn singing. Mary Lay, a great granddaughter of Edmund, recently observed that in 1844 Edmund was only eighteen years of age. By 1852 an organ had been installed in the church gallery.

THE BRITISH SCHOOL

Although the term of Revd Hopwood in Thatcham was relatively short, it was notable for the building of the British School at a cost of £1,600. This was largely due to John and Sarah Barfield, who lived nearby at *The Priory*. By a conveyance dated 29th July 1846, two freehold cottages and one leasehold cottage, together with gardens, were transferred from John Barfield to nine trustees as "a site for a School for poor persons of and in the Parishes of Thatcham, Bucklebury and other adjoining Parishes". The lease on the site of the one cottage expires in 2681. Sarah Barfield (John's third wife) was, according to Revd Summers "a talented and energetic lady, who is said to have collected £300 at Liverpool alone. It is said that after some difficulty she secured an interview with the great Duke of Wellington and appealed to him for help on the ground of the nearness of Thatcham to his estates. On the Duke addressing her with the words, 'Pray be seated, madam', she answered with ready tact, 'I could not think of sitting down in the presence of so great a man'. She then explained her errand, on which the Duke exclaimed, 'All the people in the country expect me to build their schools for them!' He gave her, however, a cheque for £5."

The British School opened in September 1847. Mrs Sarah Barfield was manager of the school from its inception until 1852. At that time there were over one hundred pupils on roll. In 1874 the school became a public elementary school and henceforth received a grant from the Government. William Brown was then the master at the school, while his brother Thomas Henry Brown was a monitor and later became a pupil-teacher there. On 27th March 1882 Horatio Barton Skillman took over as master. In 1902 His Majesty's Inspectors reported that the school was taught with industry and skill with excellent order being maintained.

THATCHAM UNDENOMINATIONAL SCHOOL 168

In 1907 the British School secretary (Mr T H Brown) reported that "in future the school would be known officially as the Thatcham Undenominational School Number 168". By 1909 the average attendance at the school had reached 150 but in December that year the managers of the school had met a school inspector, a medical inspector, a buildings inspector and the County Secretary with reference to defects in the school buildings, namely defective light and ventilation (costing £400 - £500 to make good), overcrowding and inadequate playground area. The managers decided that they could not raise the money and resolved to ask the County Council "to take over the school at an agreed rent". By April 1911 the County Council had declined to take over the school owing to the limited nature of the site. Instead a new school was built. It was opened on 1st April 1913. Mr Skillman and his four assistants transferred there. The new school was known as the Council School until 1964, when the name 'Francis Baily Primary School' was adopted.

REVD EBENEZER WHITE (1849-1859)

There were twelve applications for the ministerial vacancy in 1849. Ebenezer White of Andover was invited to come and preach, firstly on Sunday 24th

June 1849 but it was not until 20th October in that year that he was formally invited to become the pastor. His salary was set at £20 per annum "payable from the rents of the sittings, with the benefit of any excess that may be desired from that source, in addition to which there is the minister's house".

Ebenezer White, formerly a deacon of the Independent Church, Andover, was ordained "Pastor of the Congregational Church, Thatcham" on 24th April 1850. After the ordination service a large party dined together in the British School. Ebenezer appears to have made quite an impression in Thatcham. Membership of the church increased by 50% during his first year here. There were twenty-two members listed in December 1849. This had risen to thirty-three by January 1851. At the latter date the following were listed as members - John Adnams, Mrs Adnams, Mrs Allen, John Barfield (deacon), Sarah Barfield, Thomas Burgess, Ann Carter, John Carter, James Child, John Collins, John Drinkwater (deacon), George Emmans, Mr Ford, Thomas Giles, Mary Giles, John Harper, Mrs Harper, Matilda Hopwood, Mrs R Hunt, Mrs Keen, Ann Longman, Lydia Marshall, Mary Mathews, Mrs Minchin, Mrs Northway, Sarah Pinnock, Edmund Pinnock, Stephen Pinnock, Ann Tull, Richard Tull, Mr Watson, Mrs Watson and Sarah White.

Ebenezer had a varied life - at an early stage he was destined for the ministry in the Church of England but abandoned his studies at Queen's College, Oxford, to enter the merchant navy and travelled widely, including in South America and China. He eventually settled at Andover as a school teacher and became a member of the Independent Church there. He is said to have become an amateur doctor, dispensing free medical advice to the poor of Thatcham.

JOHN BARFIELD DIES, NEW DEACONS APPOINTED

It was during Ebenezer White's ministry in Thatcham that the founder of the Independent Chapel, John Barfield, died on 5th July 1851. Four days later he was buried under the pulpit in the chapel. Only two deacons had been appointed at this time - John Barfield had been one and the other was John Drinkwater, who was elderly (about eighty-six). On 31st October 1851 Messrs John Adnams and Edward Hunt were appointed as deacons. Mr Hunt did not become a church member until January 1851, although he appears to have played a leading role in church affairs prior to that time. Mr Adnams' membership was transferred from Mortimer in November 1850.

WE HAVE A CHURCH ORGAN

On 30th July 1852, the church meeting agreed that a private collection be made for the past services of Mr Terry, the organist. It was also agreed that 40/- be given out of the "Incidental Fund" to Mr Terry and that he be requested to continue as organist. Furthermore, members agreed that he should receive a sum of 40/- annually from the same fund. Subsequently Mr Terry was given a total of £4-10-0 (the 40/- plus 50/- from the private collection) but he expressed dissatisfaction with this and sent in his resignation.

During 1852-53 there was a regular weekday evening service at 7 pm, except during December and January, when it began at 6:30 pm.

John Drinkwater, a deacon of this church for nearly twelve years, died on Thursday, 26th May 1853 at the age of eighty-eight. He was buried in the churchyard of St Mary's Parish Church, Thatcham.

On 4th June 1855, the Finance Committee resolved that Mr Ellson ask "two shillings for each sitting in the middle pews of the chapel" and "that one shilling be asked for each sitting in the side pews of the chapel". The front pews and the gallery were to be five shillings.

In May 1856 the church meeting was concerned about "the mode of warming the chapel". In October that same year, it was decided "to take the necessary measures for warming the chapel" and by 30th January 1857 a stove had been installed under the direction of deacon Edward Hunt - it was considered to have met the heating need satisfactorily.

TOO MUCH LIGHT COMING IN THROUGH THE WINDOWS

In July 1857 Some members of the congregation had complained to the minister "of the inconvenience produced by the light from the windows on either side of the pulpit". Furthermore, sunlight from the window behind the organ (in the gallery) was believed to be adversely affecting the instrument so Edward Hunt was requested to get some blinds and have the window behind the organ darkened or blocked.

The church meeting agreed on 30th October 1857 "that the pew opener be authorized to fill up, after the singing of the first hymn, those pews that may be unoccupied".

On 1st April 1859 Edward Hunt resigned his position as deacon after serving for 7½ years.

Ebenezer White had served ten years as pastor in Thatcham, when he died on 27th November 1859, aged forty-five. A note in the church minute book records that "he was greatly endeared to his people". He was buried at Norwood Cemetery, London. There is a plaque to his memory in the church at Thatcham - it is fixed to the north wall of the 'chancel'.

REVD CHARLES GOWAR (1861-1872)

In December 1859 the church advertised for "a Minister to take the oversight of the Congregational Church at Thatcham", where the members and congregation were "a very united but poor people". The minister's salary was to be £20 per annum plus an endowment of about £30.

From a "considerable number" of applicants, Revd Thomas Islip, the Revd Thomas Davies and the Revd I A Merrington were invited to come and preach.

Apparently all came and preached but "neither of them were accepted by the Church". The Revd Thomas Moody of Charlton Adam (Somerset) was then invited to preach for two Sabbaths and was subsequently invited to take the ministry for a probationary period of six calendar months with a view to taking the pastorate thereafter. He accepted in a letter dated 2nd April 1860 and took up residence at *The Manse* in Back Lane (24 Park Lane). In December 1860 a special church meeting was called "for the purpose of deciding whether or not Mr Moody should be invited to be the Minister and Pastor of the Church". The votes were counted as follows, viz: For Mr Moody 5, Against 16. Following that vote, a canvass of the communicants taken on 5th and 6th February 1861, produced the result as follows: For Mr Moody 3, Against 23, Neutrals 6, Not contacted 5. Revd Moody appears to have ministered for a little over eight months, leaving early in 1861.

In March 1861 a church management committee, consisting of Messrs John Adnams, William Casson, Edmund Pinnock and Thomas Pinnock, was set up. Its first task was to find a prospective pastor. Revd Charles Gowar of Upwey, near Weymouth, Dorset, was invited to preach on the first two Sabbaths in April. This he did and must have made a good impression on members because two months later, they voted by 16-3 to offer him the pastorship. He accepted in June 1861.

A system of pew renting was then in operation - the collector at this time was Edmund Pinnock, who expressed his wish to discontinue the collecting of the rents. Edmund recommended his brother Samuel as a suitable person to take the office and this was agreed at a church meeting in June 1861.

AVERAGE CONGREGATION WAS 185

A statistical return made to the secretary of the Congregational County Union in June 1861 reveals that the church was still being referred to as Thatcham Independent Chapel. It belonged to the Newbury Union. The number of sittings (seats) was 225 (of which about one third was free), while the average congregation was given as 185. Church members numbered 39, Sunday School scholars 60 and Sunday School teachers 8.

SUSPENDED FOR SIN COMMITTED AGAINST GOD

At the church meeting on 4th October 1862, it was unanimously agreed that Mr John Brown be "suspended from fellowship for six months to allow space for repentance". He was informed of this decision by letter, as follows - "My Dear Sir, It is with much regret I have the painful duty to say that a report has been laid before the Church in assembly that you have been dismissed from Mr Shaw's service for taking his wood. Enquiry has been made of Mr Shaw and it has been found true, in consequence of which I have to inform you that they (the church members) have decided that you be suspended from Church fellowship for six months during which period they trust you may be led to see the Sin committed against God and repent of it and obtain mercy of the Lord. I remain, Yours truly, Charles Gowar, Pastor."

BICENTENARY YEAR CELEBRATED

A note in the church minute book refers to the Bicentenary Year of 1862. On Sunday 24th August 1862, two sermons were preached in celebration. The morning text was 'We ought to obey God rather than Man' and the evening text - 'The Righteous shall be in everlasting remembrance'. It was on this date in 1662 that Revd Thomas Voisey was ejected from his living as Vicar of St Mary's Parish Church, Thatcham, because of his Puritanism and his stand for 'liberty of conscience' (see pages 13-15).

At the church meeting of 4th December 1863, it was decided that "something should be given weekly to the boy who blows the bellows for the organ, say one penny or so".

GAS HEATING INSTALLED

On 4th November 1864 members considered "the subject of the introduction of gas into the Chapel and how to pay for it" and on 2nd December 1864 "it was unanimously decided that as there had been two explosions with the hotwater apparatus" thereby damaging the property, the old piping should be sold and the proceeds used for improvements to the building then taking place, namely, the installation of gas heating and the whitewashing of the ceiling and walls. Three years later a new gas fire was installed in the vestry. Total cost of the two gas fires, piping, chimney and installation was £13-14-2.

In March 1865 Mr and Mrs John Henry were admitted to full communion on transfer from the Camden Road Congregational Church, Holloway, London.

In June 1866 the total number of church members was thirty-five plus five occasional communicants.

It was agreed in July 1867 that if any member be absent from holy communion for nine months without a satisfactory reason, he or she will be considered as having voluntarily withdrawn fellowship and would be removed from the list of members in full communion.

MEMBERSHIP THIRTY-FOUR

As at Midsummer 1867, the "Church Members in Full Communion" were John Adnams (deacon), Mrs John Adnams, Mrs Arnold, Miss Bailing, Miss Betteridge, Mrs Child, Mrs Collins, Mrs Duckett, Mr and Mrs E J Deverell, Mr Emmans, Revd C Gowar (Pastor), Mr & Mrs Gray, Mr & Mrs Harper, Miss Sarah Harper, Mr & Mrs John Henry, Mrs James Hyde, Mrs Northway, Mr Lewis, Mrs Pinnock, Stephen Pinnock, Edmund Pinnock, Mr & Mrs Thomas Pinnock, Alfred Pinnock, Mrs Smith, Mr Stair, Miss O Tennant, Mrs Wells, George Wickens and Mrs Wyles. The total of these members is thirty-four. Occasional Communicants - James Child (Baptist, Newbury), Mrs Samuel Pinnock (Independent, Newbury), Mrs Gowar (Independent, Greenwich Road).

On 1st January 1868 there was "A Church Meeting but no business". This is the entire minute record for the meeting.

As at 2nd February 1871 the chapel was insured to the value of £500, the organ at £100 and the minister's house at £400. Total value of all three was therefore £1,000.

Charles Gowar's place of birth was given as Greenwich, Kent, in the 1871 census. He was then a widower, aged fifty-four, living in *The Manse*, Back Lane (Park Lane), Thatcham. According to Revd Summers, Charles was "quiet, cautious and in very delicate health". His wife, Harriet, died while here in Thatcham. She was buried in the Newtown Road cemetery, Newbury, on 10th September 1870. Just over one year later (5th November 1871), Revd Charles Gowar gave notice of his intention to resign the pastorate as from the last Sunday in March 1872. He then spent eight years (1873-81) as pastor of the Congregational Chapel at Bucklebury. Following that he preached occasionally for a few years as required, depending on the state of his health. He died, aged seventy, on 13th April 1887 at Thatcham after a prolonged period of illness. He was buried in the same grave as his wife in Newbury.

REVD WILLIAM MILLS ROBINSON (1873-1880)

By September 1872 both Thomas Storey and Walter Greig had responded to invitations to visit Thatcham Congregational Church and each of them had preached on two Sundays. Members then voted in favour of inviting Revd Walter Greig of Huddersfield to serve a six-month probation period. This he accepted in October that year and duly served for six months. Towards the end of that time members and congregation voted overwhelmingly (70-10) to invite Revd Greig to become pastor of the church. However, in April 1873 Walter Greig respectfully declined the invitation on account of his ill health.

Soon after that Revd William Mills Robinson was invited to 'preach with a view' and by "the unanimous wish of all" members and adherents in August 1873, Revd W Mills Robinson was invited to be the new minister. There does not appear to have been a probationary period - Revd Mills Robinson commenced his ministry here on 5th October that year and was inducted at what was termed a "recognition service" on Wednesday 12th November 1873. Tea was provided in the British School at 5 pm prior to the church service at 6:30 pm. The school room was lit with gas for the first time, the fittings for which had been given by John Henry of Colthrop House.

Revd W M Robinson was stated in the church minute book as coming to Thatcham from Ross. No county was mentioned but it was probably Ross-on-Wye, Herefordshire, because in April 1881, just after he had left Thatcham, he was living in Monmouth (only ten miles from Ross-on-Wye) with two of his daughters, Alice (aged twenty-three) and Jessie (aged twelve). Furthermore, Ross-on-Wye was formerly referred to simply as Ross and that town is considerably larger than the other half-dozen or so places which have the same name. However, William Mills Robinson was born in Maidenhead, Berkshire, probably in 1819.

IMPROVEMENTS TOWARDS RITUALISM?

About sixty were present at the church meeting held on 2nd January 1874 in the British School. With Mr John Henry in the chair, Revd Robinson sought to elicit opinions concerning use of the Lord's Prayer during worship and whether the congregation desired to join in audibly. He also broached the idea of introducing the singing of a chant taken from the Scriptures. It may be difficult for us to understand nowadays but the Lord's Prayer was originally regarded by the Separatists as too ritualistic. The next recorded mention of this subject occurred at a church meeting in September 1875, when "some conversation" took place "respecting the use of the Lord's Prayer, which ended in an expression of opinion that the use of it be continued" although the congregation would not join in audibly.

It was also at the meeting of 2nd January 1874 that Mr Henry presented an architect's plan for alterations to the chapel. This embraced the removal of the greater part of the eastern wall of the chapel and "the erection of a chancel on the site of the present vestry". A platform about two feet from the floor, on which the organ and benches for the singers and a desk for the minister would be placed, was also shown. It was thought that the building work, together with "some improvements in the body of the church" and repairs of the roof would cost about £200. After much discussion, in which "one or two members expressed fears of a tendency towards Ritualism", it was agreed that the work should commence when £150 had been raised.

By 29th April 1874, the amount credited to the Restoration Fund was £261-8-3. It transpired, however, that the final cost of restoration and enlargement was £500-11-11 but by January 1877 the money had been raised and all expenses paid.

RESTORATION AND ENLARGEMENT COMPLETED

A contemporary report informs us that the alterations "consisted in taking down the eastern wall, throwing an ornamental arch across the building and taking in the old vestry, which has added 14 ft by 16 ft to the length of the edifice. In this chancel is a raised platform, upon which has been placed the present organ, which has been removed from the gallery and re-tuned. Open ornamental benches are introduced for the choir and the lofty pulpit has been superseded by a convenient desk for the preacher. At the foot of the platform is a large and substantial communion table with suitable chairs for ministers and deacons. The chancel has an opened timbered roof, stained and varnished and the new seats are of pitch pine, highly stained and varnished. The addition to the length of he building, with the increased accommodation in the gallery consequent upon the removal of the organ, has added some fifty seats, which were needed, as the whole of the sittings were previously occupied. All the old pews have been remodelled and the additional benches have been made to correspond with the new. Over the organ in the chancel, a very pretty stained glass window has been placed and the windows on either side are glazed with cathedral plain glass of a green tint."

The report also mentioned that "the pews in the old building were strictly after the type of the past century, with straight backs and narrow seats, whilst in others much room was wasted. Immediately facing the congregation on either side of the pulpit were two very large windows, which much interfered with the comfort of the worshippers on account of the strong glare of light."

It appears then that some of the present-day pews date from 1874. It is evident, however, that all the original pews (suitably remodelled) were incorporated into the present lay-out. Some of the original pews were equipped with doors and those doors were probably removed at this time. The two windows in the eastern wall of the nave also date from 1874, although the glass in those windows was originally all colourless.

At a social meeting on 1st July 1874, the "Superintendent of Sabbath School Mr Thomas Pinnock and the Master of the Day School Mr William Brown both gave cheering accounts of the increase in numbers" attending their respective schools.

REOPENING SERVICE

The Reopening Services of the church were held on Tuesday, 22nd September 1874, when the Revd W Braden of the Weigh House Church, London, preached "a most impressive sermon" and Revd J B Crowther conducted the devotional parts of the service. There were large congregations at both services, the evening service being "crowded to excess". Attendance at the tea was so large that two sittings had to be organized.

During March 1875 special services were held over eight days "commencing Lord's Day March 14th and ending on the 21st, commencing each week evening at 7:30 ...Wesleyans, Primitives, Baptists and Congregationalists joined in earnest prayers on Thursday". Ministers from all these faith groups took part. "On Friday evening the church was completely filled on the ground floor. Attendances throughout the week were most cheering and it is believed some good was done by this unusual effort to reach our fellow men."

Revd Marcus Hopwood (pastor of our church during 1843-49) took the service on Sunday 19th September 1875. He was warmly welcomed by members of the congregation, several of whom could recall "his ministrations in this church thirty years ago".

Mr John Adnams of Harts Hill Farm, who was elected deacon in October 1851 died on 6th October 1875, aged eighty-six, "a good man, full of the Holy Spirit and of Faith".

The total number of members as at March 1876 was fifty-two but attendances at church meetings that year were not very good. On 2nd February, the minister and seven members attended: on 3rd May the minister was accompanied by fourteen members and on 31st May by six. In September that year the treasurer (Thomas Pinnock) gave his half-yearly financial report: the total income for the six months to June 1876 was £66-15-5, an increase of £5-19-9 on the previous six months. There was "such a goodly balance" on the account that members presented £5 to the minister, Revd Robinson.

SARAH BARFIELD CALLED HOME

On Sunday 14th October 1877, Mrs Sarah Barfield, widow of John Barfield and formerly of *The Priory*, "was called home after some nine months suffering". On the following Sunday evening, Revd W Mills Robinson preached with "reference to her long connection with this Christian Church, her life of active usefulness and Christian charity and her most peaceful departure". Mrs Barfield was instrumental in raising the £1,600 for the building of the British School and the £500 for the enlargement of the chapel "but in very many ways and for a long course of years proved herself to be a most generous and practical friend to the Church of Christ in this Parish and a 'fellow helper' in all good works".

George Emmans, who started attending this church sometime between 1813 and 1820, died 30th June 1879, aged eighty-two. He was "an old disciple, very constant ... a teacher in the Sunday School until he was seventy-eight years of age".

Thomas Pinnock, deacon, organist and superintendent of the Sunday School for many years, died on 30th June 1880. He was church organist from 1852 and a church member from 1859.

MYSTERIOUS CONVICTION

At a church meeting on 18th June 1880, with John Henry in the chair and twenty-six members present, it was revealed that there was a "conviction resting upon the mind of the Minister - gathered from a statement publicly made by him on Lord's Day 23rd May". The Committee of Management believed that "it would tend to the welfare of the Church if Mr Robinson sought some other sphere of service". A free and open discussion followed, after which members agreed "That Mr Robinson quietly and peaceably resign the pastorate of this Church forthwith and in consideration firstly, this Church agree to pay Mr Robinson three months salary in advance (up to the 29th day of September 1880) - which including pew rents and endowment would be about £22-10-0". This was accepted by Mr Robinson. The conviction resting upon his mind has to remain a mystery. The suggestion that he seek "some other sphere of service" may indicate that he was having serious doubts about his Christian faith. It may, on the other hand, merely indicate a conviction to preach elsewhere.

EDWARD JENKIN GRIFFITHS (1881-1899)

On 10th August 1881 members decided to ask Mr E J Griffiths of Petersfield to preach the Sunday School's annual sermon. His sermon must have been impressive for on the basis of that, members "unanimously resolved to invite the Revd E J Griffiths to take the oversight of the Church", subject to further enquiries being made at Petersfield by Edmund Pinnock on behalf of the church. The enquiries produced satisfactory information for on 17th September 1881, Revd E J Griffiths was invited to accept the pastorate at Thatcham, with the option of "three months notice on either side". He accepted the invitation but was rather concerned that the church could "only raise £90". However, his experience in Petersfield encouraged him to hope that Thatcham might be able to do better in the future than it had in the past. He related how in Petersfield he had persuaded members to abandon the 'pew rent system' in favour of a 'weekly offering system'. Some members there thought the minister would be the loser but it transpired that the weekly offering system raised more money and his salary had averaged about £130 per annum as against the £90 per annum received at Petersfield under its pew rent system.

Revd Griffiths appears to have commenced his ministry at Thatcham on Sunday 6th November 1881. On Wednesday of the following week, tea was provided in the British School to enable members and the congregation to meet their new minister informally.

Edward Jenkin Griffiths was born at Aberdare (Glamorgan) on 27th March 1839. He left his native Wales as a young man to become a gold-miner in Australia. He did not, evidently, find satisfaction in that field for he enrolled as one of the first students in the Congregational College at Melbourne and stayed in Australia to hold three pastorates in Victoria (Ross Creek, Ballarat and Landsborough). On returning to his homeland in 1872 he settled in North Wales. After three years there he moved to Petersfield (Hampshire) and thence to Thatcham.

STEPHEN RAY PINNOCK APPOINTED AS SECRETARY

It seems that until this time, it was customary for the minister to act as secretary for the church. Shortly after Revd Griffiths had settled here, he requested that some other person take on that role. Accordingly, Stephen Ray Pinnock was unanimously elected as church secretary on 28th December 1881.

Revd E J Griffiths was inducted at a "recognition service" in Thatcham on Monday, 30th January 1882. At a church meeting on 31st May 1882, Mr H B Skillman and Mrs Harriet Pinnock were received into church membership.

On the resignation of John Henry as church treasurer, Edmund Pinnock "being the oldest member of the Church" was appointed as treasurer on 3rd January 1883.

On 8th August 1883, Mr John Henry resigned his office as an active deacon "pleading his inability to attend the meetings and also his frequent absence from home". He continued for nearly eight more years as a 'non-serving deacon'.

On 28th November 1883, Mr & Mrs H S Peters, Frederick James Reynolds, Ada Pinnock, Bertha Wheeler and Amy Whiting were received into church membership. In the following January, Samuel Pocock, Mr B Child, Mr & Mrs Charles Brown also became members.

Church meetings, which were held every four weeks at this time, were not always very busy affairs during 1884. Those held on the following dates in that year - 2nd July, 30th July, 3rd September, 1st October and 29th October, were all recorded simply as having "no business".

On 31st December 1884, Mrs Salatina Skillman and Thomas Henry Brown were received into church membership.

FAREWELL TO PEW RENTS

At a special church meeting held on 9th June 1886 members agreed to give the weekly offering system a fair trial, which if successful, would thereby replace the pew rent system. Mr Skillman was appointed to approach the members and seat holders to ascertain the amount of support a weekly offering would most likely receive before it be finally adopted. Eleven weeks later, members agreed to adopt the weekly offering system from the beginning of the next quarter. At the end of 1886 there were fifty-four church members.

Stephen Ray Pinnock, having just resigned as secretary, was replaced by Mr W H Bebbington in March 1888. Towards the end of 1888, the church rules were amended and 100 copies were printed so that each member could have a copy.

TWO OFFENDING MEMBERS

In November 1888 the pastor, Revd Griffiths, stated "that he was sorry to have to refer to the conduct of certain members of the church (Mr and Mrs Woodhouse) - whose manner of living was not in accordance with their profession as Christians and he thought that the church was called upon to notice the same". It was agreed that the pastor seek an interview with them and report back. The pastor reported back that same month - the result of his interview was that the two offending members - after careful consideration of the matter by the meeting, were "requested to abstain from the Lord's Table for two months".

As a result of an inspiring talk at a recent church meeting, a local branch of the Temperance Society was formed in November 1890. Mr Mark Knowles of London promised to give a lecture in connection with the society at an early date.

At the end of 1889 sixty-nine members were listed on the church roll. In January 1891 Mr William H Bebbington resigned as church secretary. Edmund Pinnock (already the treasurer) was appointed to take Mr Bebbington's place. John Henry resigned as a deacon in April 1891.

COME FORWARD AND SIT TOGETHER PLEASE

At the Annual Social Gathering on 24th February 1892, it was thought that the Wednesday evening prayer meeting might be improved in interest by the congregation "coming forward and sitting together and not sit as they now do, one here and there all over the place".

It was reported on 1st February 1893 that a thermometer had recently been bought at a cost of one shilling.

TWO NEW DEACONS ELECTED

On 3rd April 1895 Horatio Skillman and James Couzens were elected as deacons. There were three other candidates who took part in the election, namely - Stephen Ray Pinnock, Charles Brown and Thomas Henry Brown.

NEW SECRETARY APPOINTED

On 1st May 1895 the deacons "met in accordance with a resolution of the church to choose a (new) secretary from their own body". It is apparent that since 1891 Edmund Pinnock had been serving as both secretary and treasurer, even though the merging of the two roles into one was deemed inadvisable at a church meeting in March 1893. At the meeting in May 1895 Mr H Skillman was appointed as church secretary.

In June 1896 the pastor announced that, in accordance with a decision made the previous year, he had granted permission to the Primitive Methodists the use of our chapel for their anniversary services.

In March 1897 Thomas Henry Brown proposed that on alternate Sunday evenings the congregation be invited to remain after the service to sing hymns. The object of his proposal was "to induce the congregation to take a greater interest in the singing and thus improve the praise portion of the service of God".

EDMUND PINNOCK, A MEMBER FOR FIFTY-THREE YEARS

In October 1898 Arthur Brown agreed to take on the role of church treasurer from Edmund Pinnock, who wished to resign owing to his failing health. Edmund, a deacon and former Sunday School teacher, died on 30th November 1898. He had been a member of the church since 1845.

Reverend Griffiths was the resident minister here for just over seventeen years. According to Thomas H Brown, his ministry here was quiet but it had a "true spiritual power which made the period one of growth in the deepest life of the church". Aged fifty-nine, he died on 16th February 1899 after severe suffering and is buried in Thatcham cemetery. There is a road, Griffiths Close (off Agricola Way) in Thatcham named after Revd Griffiths.

It was decided in April 1899 that from that time all deacons would be elected every three years. The diaconate from May that year comprised Arthur Brown, James Couzens, Henry Shepherd and Horatio Skillman.

JASPER J FREWING (1900-1906)

In June 1899 two prospective pastors were invited to preach here - Revds H Russell of Caversham and E J Hunt of Fordingbridge. Following their visits to Thatcham, both these gentlemen were given due consideration by members, who failed to reach a positive decision and instead invited Revd Jasper J Frewing of Faringdon, Berkshire, to 'preach with a view'. In November 1899 members decided by 20 votes out of 23 to invite Jasper Frewing to become pastor for a term of five years, subject to renewal. He started his ministry here on 4th February 1900. Membership then numbered seventy-three.

On 5th December 1899, it was reported that for each of the past four years, the total collections for the ministerial fund were £50-12-11, £54-18-5, £54-16-5 and £54-8-6.

The new church organ, 1905.
This picture appeared in Revd Summers' booklet, produced to mark the centenary
of Thatcham Congregational Church.

Jasper Frewing, son of Henry and Emma Frewing, was born at Great Marlow (now called Marlow), Buckinghamshire, in 1864/5. His wife's name was Maria. A son of theirs, named Jasper, was born in Thatcham in 1900.

DISORDER IN THE GALLERY

Arthur Brown had cause in October 1900 to refer to "the disorderly conduct of some lads in the gallery on Sunday evenings and requested the pastor to speak to them from the desk. The pastor pointed out the danger that might arise from so doing but thought that an appeal to them in a kindly spirit would be productive of good."

It was at this time that John Henry was urging the building of additional space for the school. However, it was not until April 1903 that a special meeting was called to consider a plan initiated by Mr Henry for the building of class rooms to the front of the chapel. The estimated cost was £230. A committee was to consider the matter. Needless to say, the proposal was never pursued, partly because of the existence of graves under the lawn at the front of the church.

In April 1904 Revd Frewing was reappointed for another five years: of sixty possible votes there were forty-nine in favour and only six against.

CENTURY UP AND A NEW ORGAN

In November 1904 Arthur Brown was urging the purchase of a new organ, the cost of which was expected to be about £150: the existing organ could be sold for £15. A new organ was duly purchased and officially brought into use on Wednesday, 29th March 1905, when the Mayoress of Newbury, Mrs Hopson, was in attendance. There was a large congregation for the occasion. The organist at that time was Thomas Henry Brown, who resigned from the post in 1906.

It was around this time that Revd W H Summers of Hungerford was completing his *History of the Congregational Churches in the Berks, South Oxon and*

South Bucks Association. The book was published in 1905 and Revd Summers kindly had the Thatcham section of it copied and bound separately to mark the centenary of Thatcham Congregational Church.

DEATH OF JOHN HENRY

In 1905 members were saddened to hear of the death of John Henry of Colthrop. A letter of condolence was sent to Mrs Henry. John died on 23rd October that year. Born in Glasgow in 1823, John Henry moved from London to Colthrop in 1861 and rented the paper mill there from William Mount (junior). In about 1864 he bought the mill. There is a plaque to the memory of John and his wife Anne on the south wall of the church.

In July 1906, Revd Frewing presented a letter of his resignation to the church meeting. It was accepted by members with appreciation of "his faithful service and their earnest wish that the blessing of our Heavenly Father would attend him in his new sphere of labour".

Revd Frewing last preached here on Sunday 30th September 1906. A presentation was made by the congregation - it consisted of a study chair and bible to Mr Frewing and an occasional chair to Mrs Frewing together with "a purse of gold containing £18". Membership totalled seventy-nine in January 1907.

JESSE GEORGE DAVIS (1907-1917)

After preaching here 'with a view', Revd J G Phillips, was invited in February 1907 to become pastor: this was agreed unanimously but the enthusiasm was not mutual for the following month Revd Phillips declined the invitation.

It was then that Jesse George Davis, student of New College, London, came to preach and was subsequently invited to become the pastor. As a student, Jesse Davis had preached here some years earlier for Revd Frewing. Jesse was born in 1878 at Faringdon, Berkshire, son of George and Mary Davis. He first joined the Congregational Church shortly before 1896 at Coleraine, Northern Ireland, where he took an interest in Sunday School and mission work, following which he enrolled for a ministry course at New College, London, where he spent six years. In April 1901, Jesse Davis was living at Sherington, Buckinghamshire: he was then aged twenty-two and described in the census at that time as a Congregational student.

A PREACHER OF NO MEAN ORDER

Jesse began his ministry in Thatcham in August 1907 and was ordained here on Wednesday, 20th November 1907. Miss Katie Carter was the organist. Following the ordination service, the church secretary, Horatio Skillman, described Revd Davis as "a preacher of no mean order. His sermons were short; they were prepared with very great care and yet they did not smell of the study too much. They were distinctly original."

Revd Davis' remuneration was agreed as £40 per annum, together with weekly offerings allocated to the ministerial fund plus half the loose money in the offerings plus the whole collection taken at the annual anniversary service. He was also entitled to four Sundays off each year.

MONSTROUS EVIL OF INTEMPERANCE

In April 1908 members decided to organize a united meeting of the Free Churches in support of the Licensing Bill before Parliament. Mr Peters, who was to represent this church, was instructed to convey to the Free Church Council the earnest wish of Thatcham Congregational Church that it would "do all in its power to support the Government in its temperance legislation". The consumption of alcohol was evidently a serious social problem at the time. In his *Oxford History of England*, Sir Robert Ensor refers to "the then monstrous evil of intemperance". Notwithstanding that King Edward VII and the Church of England supported the 1908 Licensing Bill, it was rejected by the House of Lords.

British School pupils with headteacher Horatio Skillman, about 1911. Picture - courtesy of Mary Lay.

On 5th January 1909 Mr Skillman spoke of the "very poor attendance" at the church meeting that evening. Members subsequently agreed to return to the former practice of holding church meetings immediately after the week night service.

FRIENDLY RELATIONS WITH THE GERMANS

In November 1909 the Congregational Union wrote on the matter of German pastors visiting England and "the desire of the churches to strive to maintain friendly relations between the two nations". Members supported this unanimously.

In February 1910 it was announced that James Couzens, a teacher in the Sunday School for more than forty-one years was "desirous of retiring".

In July 1912 a "desultory discussion ensued on the old question of putting windows in the north wall of the chapel". It was considered inadvisable to incur further expense at that time (see March 1921).

On 6th May 1913, the following deacons were elected unopposed - Messrs Arthur Brown, James Couzens, Horatio Skillman and Frederick James Reynolds. In addition Mr Robert Vincent was made (as in the case of the late Mr John Henry) "a deacon of the church but relieved from the duties and responsibilities of that office" - effectively he became a non-serving deacon.

GLARE OF LIGHT FROM THE WINDOWS

In June 1914 complaints were made about "the glare of light from the windows" - this must have referred to light from the windows at the eastern end of the church, because at that time there were no windows in the north or south walls.

DEATH OF STEPHEN RAY PINNOCK

Also in June 1914 members heard of "the great loss which our church has sustained in the death of Stephen Ray Pinnock, who for many years was one of our most honoured members and for a period (1881-88) our church secretary". Stephen Ray Pinnock became a church member in July 1874. His grandmother Sarah Pinnock and his father Stephen Pinnock were both members before him, as were his uncles Edmund (church treasurer and secretary) and Thomas Pinnock (church treasurer and organist). Stephen Ray died on 11th June 1914, aged sixty-four. He is buried in Thatcham cemetery.

At the church meeting of 9th February 1915 Thomas Henry Brown was appointed as Temperance secretary.

In November 1915 the pastor stated that "complaints had been made by members of the church about the conduct of boys who come to the evening service unattended by their parents". Revd Davis, who did not want to exclude them, must have been grateful when "a number of members offered to allow one or two boys to be put into their pews".

Also at that time members agreed "to co-operate with our Wesleyan friends" in arranging something for the soldiers during their stay in the village. A Free Church Committee was appointed last year to consider this.

NEED FOR MORE WINDOWS
In February 1916 Arthur Brown urged the church to consider "putting additional windows in the building". The possibility of acquiring a piece of land at the back of the chapel and of enlarging the chapel was also suggested.

NO LEGAL CLAIM TO STRIP OF LAND
In June 1916 Revd Davis reported that the church had just paid £50 for a strip of land five feet wide on the south side of the chapel (land formerly owned by the church but "for so many years in the undisputed possession of the late occupier of the adjacent property that we no longer had any legal claim to it") and a piece eighteen feet wide at the eastern end of the chapel.

On 30th January 1917 Robert Vincent kindly volunteered to distribute the church magazines and was duly appointed magazine secretary. He carried out this task for three years.

On 29th May 1917 Thomas H Brown suggested that the national anthem be sung at Sunday evening services but "in view of the smallness of the attendance at the church meeting, it was deemed inadvisable to proceed".

On Sunday 23rd September 1917, the pastor announced that he had accepted an invitation from the church at Melbourn, Cambridgeshire, to become its pastor. His pastorate here would end on 21st October 1917. There were eighty-nine members on the roll in January 1918.

Revd Jesse G Davis was married and had one child, a daughter named Alma. The family lived at *The Manse*, 24 Park Lane. Denise Cochrane recently recalled that Alma, who became a school teacher, remained a great friend of Marjorie Brown (daughter of Arthur Brown) and regularly visited Marjorie after moving away from Thatcham. On retirement from teaching, Alma, who never married, went to live at Axminster, Devon.

REVD JOHN STAY (1918-1933)

In April 1918 members invited Revd John Stay to preach at Thatcham. For ten years previously he had been pastor at Summertown, Oxford. He was inducted at Thatcham on Wednesday 25th September 1918. A note in the minute book informs us that owing to the disorganization of railway traffic caused by the railway workers' strike, friends from Oxford were unable to be present at the ordination. Two services were held that day, one in the afternoon and another in the evening.

In October 1918 it was agreed to increase the diaconate from five (including one honorary life deacon) to nine (including two honorary life deacons), each for a term of three years - two deacons retiring after one year, two after two years and three after three years from that time.

In July 1919 the Sunday School was closed on account of an epidemic of measles. The opportunity was taken to decorate the school room and carry out some maintenance work on the church at the same time.

On 30th September 1919 Mr Lay pointed out that the current "rigid rationing" of food was likely to cause some difficulty for the forthcoming anniversary tea. The pastor agreed to discuss this matter with the food controller.

In November 1920 it was reported that a Girls' Guild had been formed and was led by Mrs Isabel Pike and Miss Helen Stay.

ADDITIONAL WINDOWS INSTALLED

On 29th March 1921 the deacons recommendation "that four windows 2½ ft by 8 ft, similar to drawings shown, should be added to the church, two in the north wall and two in the south", was considered at the church meeting. This was not the first time that the subject of additional windows had been discussed (see July 1912). The main concern at this time was whether to have iron or lead frames and the difference in cost of the two metals. By July of that year a decision had been made and the work had been entrusted to Frederick James Reynolds and his son Frederick John Reynolds (both church members) - the chapel was to be closed for two Sundays. By September 1921 the windows had been installed and general satisfaction was expressed with the work but "it now remained to make such alterations in the other windows" - in the east wall of the nave and the chancel - "so that they might agree in tone of colour with the new ones". The original windows in the old chapel consisted of plain glass while the recently installed windows in the north and south walls included the coloured glass as currently seen. When the chancel was built in 1874 three new windows were installed - the window above the organ included some coloured glass. The two side windows in the chancel were originally plain glass windows.

In 1922 the diaconate consisted of the following serving members - Miss Esther (Hettie) Peters, Arthur Brown. Thomas Henry Brown, James Couzens, Harry Carter, John H Pike and Horatio B Skillman. Church membership then numbered ninety.

VISITORS FROM AUSTRALIA

In 1922 the two plain glass windows in the east wall of the nave and the window above the organ were replaced by Mr Reynolds with the stained glass windows that currently exist. The two nave windows were paid for by members of the family of the late Mr & Mrs Jonathan and Anne Sarah Harman as a memorial to their parents, Jonathan and Anne Sarah. Memorial plaques were affixed beneath the windows and remain to this day. It should be noted here that on 21st June 2004, a note was made in the visitors' book at the URC, Thatcham, to record that "Pat and Philip Harman, Sydney, Australia, came to see the plaques for Jonathan and Sarah, grandparents". It was also decided at that time (1922) to replace the plain glass in the side windows of the chancel with stained glass in memory of Thomas and Edmund Pinnock (brothers). The new windows were eventually installed - they were dedicated on 5th October 1924, when the brass memorial plates for Thomas and Edmund were unveiled.

MEMBERSHIP TOPS ONE HUNDRED

Church membership topped the one hundred during 1922 and by the end of that year stood at 103. During 1923 however, the transfer of Mr and Mrs H B Skillman and Miss Skillman to Bridport (Dorset) and Mrs Elsie Penn to Newbury reduced that number to ninety-nine.

At the church AGM on 19th February 1924, Mr Godfrey Lay was given "a vote of thanks for his services at the organ". Also at that meeting, Miss Hettie

Peters reported that there were 102 scholars and seventeen teachers in the Sunday School at that time.

In September 1924 Miss Clara Carrington and Mrs Isabel Pike suggested the formation of a Women's Own branch in Thatcham. The Thatcham group was founded on 20th October 1924. Revd John Stay was elected as its president and Mrs Isabel Pike as its leader (superintendent registrar). There were four supporting registrars (Mrs Grace Fuller, Mrs Harding, Mrs F Ashman and Miss Hawkins).

In January 1925 Revd Stay accepted the offer from members to remain at Thatcham and declined an offer from Dursley (Gloucestershire) to transfer there.

ELECTRIC LIGHTING REPLACES GAS

In October 1925 it was agreed to have electric lighting installed in the church and in the school room. It would cost about £75 to install with an annual cost of £8 for the school and another £8 for the church. Although considerably more than gas had cost to run in the past, electricity was considered to "be cleaner, healthier and more convenient than the gas". By February 1926 electric lighting had been installed.

At the anniversary service on Wednesday 22nd September 1926, a party of Welsh miners gave musical selections between the tea and the church service, when £2-9-3½d was collected in aid of the wives and children of the miners on strike.

On 6th September 1927 members were informed that the late Matthew Henry had left £1,000 in trust to the deacons to be invested, the interest to be distributed to needy and desperate women and children, regardless of religion.

INDIVIDUAL COMMUNION CUPS INTRODUCED

In March 1929 the Revd Stay reported "that there was a general desire that the individual communion cup should be introduced and that Miss Hettie Peters had kindly offered to present two sets to the church, one in memory of

Miss Clara Carrington and the other in memory of her brother, Mr H S Peters, who was secretary of the Sunday School for many years, both to be suitably inscribed". It was agreed to adopt the change in communion practice.

On Sunday evening, 6th April 1930, the following young people from the Sunday School and Congregation were received into church membership - Stanley Brown, Stella Brown, Eric H Cass, Hilda Mary Pike, Reg E G Hart, Edna Hart, Nelly Benson, Anneeta Woodward, Gladys Green and Ellen Bertha Woodward.

DEATH OF ARTHUR BROWN

Arthur Brown, for fifty years a member of this church and superintendent of the Sunday School, a deacon (1887-1930) and church treasurer for thirty-two years, passed away on 21st October 1930, aged seventy-three. The pastor spoke of his work, of his character and of his influence for good in the district, emphasizing especially the loss the church has sustained by his passing. Fellow members stood in silence as a tribute to his memory. It was then agreed that Mr A B Vincent Brown succeed his father as deacon and treasurer. Miss Marjorie Brown (daughter of Arthur Brown) was elected superintendent of the Sunday School in succession to her father.

MEMBERSHIP REGAINS THE HUNDRED LEVEL

The Annual Church Meeting was held on 4th February 1931. Membership numbered 103 at the end of 1930 as against ninety-five the previous year. It was eight years earlier that the roll of church members reached one hundred for the first time, dipping below that level the following year. Income during 1930 was £456 and expenditure £446: there was a balance in hand of £84 as at 31st December 1930.

In March 1931, a need for further accommodation was raised. Preliminary steps were to be taken to further the building of a room and kitchen, as a memorial to the late Arthur Brown (see page 58).

*Arthur Brown, church member for fifty-years, deacon for forty-three
and treasurer for thirty-two.
Picture - courtesy of Denise Cochrane, granddaughter of Arthur.*

DEACONS BECOME TRUSTEES OF BRITISH SCHOOL

In July 1931 members agreed to ask the Congregational Union of England and Wales to accept the trusteeship of the church property in place of the one surviving trustee. The transfer of trusteeship was accepted by the Congregational Union and in January 1933 the Charity Commission confirmed the transfer. It was also announced that month that the Board of Education had agreed to the minister and deacons of the church becoming trustees of the British School in addition to their function as managers of it.

SUICIDE OF THE MINISTER

The Revd John Stay left his home on Tuesday 17th January 1933 and did not return. He was seen to board a bus bound for Reading. On the following morning his gloves and a letter written in his handwriting were discovered on the Thames promenade at Caversham. Every effort was made to trace his whereabouts and on Saturday 18th February 1933, he was found drowned in the River Thames about 450 yards from where the gloves and letter had been found. An inquest was held at Reading. The letter revealed the distracted state of Revd Stay's mind at the time. His son-in-law, Percy Pinnock, confirmed at the inquest that John Stay had been mentally depressed for some time. The verdict was "suicide whilst of unsound mind".

John Stay was sixty-four years of age. He left a widow, one son and two married daughters. John had been in the Congregational Church ministry for thirty-eight years. Some of that ministry had been at Beaconsfield, Buckinghamshire, where he also served as chairman of Beaconsfield Urban District Council. He moved from Beaconsfield to Summertown, Oxford, in 1908. Revd Stay served as general secretary of the Berks, South Oxon and South Bucks Congregational Union for twenty-three years until the day of his death. His fellow Congregationalists were full of praise for the work he did for the church "unstintingly, whole-heartedly and devotedly". Revd Stay also involved himself in village life while in Thatcham - he was president of

Tennis Group at Wetherdene (22 Park Lane), 1931.

Back Row: Stanley Brown, Wilfred Rogers, Revd John Stay, Mrs Couzens, John Morris, John H Pike, Mrs Florence Robbins, Mrs Florence Brown, Ruth Barr, Mrs Morris.

Middle Row: Mrs Amy Lay, Mildred Jarvis, Mrs Grace Fuller, Muriel Barr, Mrs Stay, Mrs Isabel Pike, Jean Pike (with the donkey), Gordon Barr and in the front: Mary Lay. Nearly all of them were Congregationalists.

Picture - courtesy of Mary Lay.

Thatcham Football Club, vice-president of Thatcham Cricket Club, a member of the Cottage Garden Society, of the Nursing Association and of the British Legion. One of his hobbies was bee-keeping, which is said to have inspired some of his sermons.

REVD ARTHUR ENFORD RICHMOND (1933-1942)

In September 1933, Revd A E Richmond, having recently preached here, was invited to take the pastorate. The church secretary at that time, Alfred Robert Brown, reported that Revd Richmond had endeared himself to all the church members. Arthur Richmond promptly accepted but because he had been offered a course at London University, for which he had been waiting five years, he wished to enrol for the course. However, he would live in Thatcham and be able to take the services each Sunday. This was accepted. Revd Richmond was inducted at Thatcham Congregational Church on Wednesday 20th December 1933.

Because Revd Richmond and his wife, Lily May, did not wish to live in *The Manse*, 24 Park Lane, it was agreed to sell it for about £650 and purchase another property in its place. In March 1934 members agreed to buy *Woodlawn* (39 Bath Road) for about £740. Apparently this was also not to the liking of Revd and Mrs Richmond, who then decided to have their own new house (*Southlands*, 466 London Road) built at Benham Hill. Until this was ready for occupation, they lived at 32 Bath Road, Thatcham.

Arthur Richmond, educated in the USA, was a graduate of Yale University (New Haven, Connecticut). He spent twelve years elsewhere in England before coming to Thatcham, having held pastorates in Bristol, Devizes and Stroud Green (London).

HE FLUNG HIMSELF ABOUT THE PULPIT

Current member Denise Cochrane recently recalled that Revd Richmond "was a little fiery man with long dark hair, who flung himself about the pulpit" when delivering a sermon. Her cousin, Robert Brown of Cold Ash recalled that this same minister taught Latin and scripture at St Batholomew's Grammar School, Newbury. Robert was one of his scripture pupils and remembers Revd Richmond "ranting and raving" at inattentive boys in class. He would chastise those who would "rather spend their time eating rhubarb and custard" than learning scripture.

In February 1935 there were ninety-seven members on roll.

LET'S GO EASY ON NEW TUNES
In September 1935 Mr Reynolds' tender of £271-4-6 for a new room (the parlour) and alterations to the vestry and the "small room in the British School" (apparently the stage area) was accepted. Members also agreed that "well known (hymn) tunes should be used more freely". It was thought "not advisable to have more than one new tune on any one Sunday".

On Wednesday 10th June 1936 the parlour was officially opened and dedicated by Revd J G Davis, former minister of our church. The ceremony was followed by a service led by Revd Davis in the afternoon.

Church members and friends suffered the loss of Mrs Hilda Robbins on 27th October 1936. Aged thirty-seven, she died after an operation in Royal Berks Hospital, Reading. Revd Richmond spoke of the "happy disposition" of Mrs Robbins and "her willing support of the church". She loved music and sang in the choir with "her beautifully soft voice". She was the wife of Henry John Robbins and the mother of Donald Robbins.

On 16th December 1936 about twenty members of Tilehurst Congregational Church visited Thatcham, "when a most interesting discussion on 'Should the Christian Church be Pacifist?' was held in the church parlour".

On 28th September 1938 it was agreed to install electric heating in the church for £71-10-0 with running cost at ¾d per unit from the Wessex Electricity Company. Electric heaters were installed shortly after that time.

DEATH OF THOMAS HENRY BROWN

Thomas Henry Brown (brother of Arthur Brown) died on 3rd May 1939, aged seventy-nine. Thomas was very knowledgeable on local history - he wrote several articles and often gave talks on it. He was a deacon of our church and served as secretary during 1923-31. He was a church organist for several years until 1906. Thomas also served on Thatcham Parish Council for forty-four years (1895-1939), which stands to this day as a record length of time for any councillor on the Parish Council.

On Wednesday, 5th July 1939 the garden was held at Wetherdene, Park Lane - the weather was showery from the start and the evening programme was spoilt by heavy rain. Nevertheless, net proceeds amounted to about £30.
The fête was opened by Mrs Summersby of Newtown Common.

THERE IS A WAR ON YOU KNOW

On 24th October 1939 Revd Richmond reported that members of the Badminton Club had offered to 'black out' the school in accordance with wartime regulations. Their offer was accepted with many thanks.

At the church meeting in the parlour on 16th January 1940, the pastor and thirteen members were present. Miss Stella Brown "asked if anything in the way of a rest room could be arranged for the soldiers billeted in the village as the only places of meeting were the public houses". It was agreed to discuss this with the other local churches. Two months later it was reported that the "soldiers rest room had proved very useful, especially for the men to write letters". It appears to have been established at the National School (St Mary's) in Park Lane. In 1942 The Women's Own undertook to take charge of it.

British School (with perimeter wall and railings) and the Congregational Church, probably in the 1930s. Picture - courtesy of John Hutchings.

In March 1940 deacons elected by ballot were Messrs A R Brown (re-elected), A B V Brown (re-elected) and H J Robbins (elected to the fill vacancy left by Thomas H Brown, who had recently died.

LET'S SING THE NATIONAL ANTHEM
On 11th June 1940 Revd Richmond's suggestion that the National Anthem be sung at the close of the morning service on the first Sunday in each month was agreed.

In July 1940 Revd Richmond reported that the choirmaster, John (Jack) Morris, would be leaving Thatcham for a time on work of national importance. It was then agreed that Mr F Wicks be asked to carry on as choirmaster.

Gabrielle Bell, one of our current members, was married to Bernard Randall in our church on 31st July 1940 by Revd Richmond. Gabrielle (known as Gay) recently recalled that it was a fine sunny day - the honeymoon was in Bournemouth. For twenty-five years from about 1948, Bernard and Gay ran a greengrocery and florist shop at 29 High Street, Thatcham.

AIR RAID ALERT PREVENTS MEETING
The church meeting arranged for 19th November 1940 "was not held owing to an air raid alert being sounded just prior to 7 pm".

On 21st January 1941 Edmund Pinnock (junior) and Henry J Robbins were both re-elected as deacons unopposed.

BRITISH SCHOOL TO BE REOPENED
On 21st October 1941 the church secretary reported that "Berkshire County Council had decided to take over the (British) School for the duration of the war at a rental of £52 pa, inclusive of fair wear and tear but exclusive of heating, lighting, cleaning and rates. These terms were agreed and the secretary

was instructed to ask that the cases of milk bottles be left inside the railings, owing to the danger to pedestrians in the dark, when left outside."

In February 1942 an application for the use of the parlour as an ARP First Aid Point was received. It was decided on the proposition of Mr A R Brown that the room "should not be let in this case".

On 21st March 1942 Mrs Esther Reynolds, Mrs Florence Robbins and John H Pike were re-elected as deacons and Albert Digweed was elected as a deacon in place of Charles G Brown.

At the church meeting on 8th April 1942, when twenty-six members were present, Mrs Isabel Pike was elected to take the chair. The main item on the agenda was a resignation letter from Revd Richmond, who gave notice that he wished to resign the pastorate at the end of April.

REVD OWEN EVAN OWEN (1943-1950)

Revd Owen of Llanelly, Wales, was invited to preach here on 28th June 1942. He preached here again shortly after that. At a church meeting on 1st October 1942, with twenty-one members present, the chairman, Mrs Reynolds, referred to a "considerable amount of doubt in the minds of members" during consideration of the appointment of a new minister. Eventually however, Revd Owen was offered the pastorship, "practically unanimously" at £5 per week on a contract of five years (extension to be decided at start of 4th year), with four Sundays off each year.

By the end of October 1942 Revd Owen had responded and was very happy to accept the invitation from Thatcham. He commenced his ministry here on Sunday 24th January 1943. His induction took place on Wednesday 10th February 1943 at 3 pm. There was "a large congregation and a most inspiring service was presided over by the Revd John Phillips (Moderator of the West

Midlands Province)". A new (third) *Manse* (69 Bath Road) was purchased for £850 at this time and later that year Revd Owen, his wife Winifred and their two daughters, Menna and Eryl, moved into it. The second *Manse* (39 Bath Road) was let at this time, never having been occupied by a minister.

Woolhampton Congregational Church was struggling and in June 1942 the members there asked for some "oversight" from Thatcham. In April the following year Thatcham members agreed to take oversight of the Woolhampton Church - Mr Owen was to take evening service there once a month for not less than £12 pa.

Mr H W Barr transferred to Hungerford Congregational Church in December 1942.

The Annual General Meeting of Thatcham Congregational Church held on 17th March 1943 attracted fifty members.

On 31st December 1943, a most successful social was held in the British School, with a very good attendance, including friends from the Thatcham Methodist Churches and also some "of our American friends". This was followed by a watchnight service in the church, when a short address was given by Revd Chaplain Roberts of the US Army.

On 2nd January 1944 Miss Grace Haley, Miss Rosemary White, Messrs Donald Robbins, Robin Brown, John Eggleton and Arthur Smith were received into church membership during the evening service. On 24th of that same month Miss Stella Brown and Mr A Robert Brown were re-elected delegates to the County Union Meetings.

On Sunday 28th May 1944 after the service, Chaplain Roberts, US Army, presented a notice board to the church to commemorate the happy times he had spent in the Thatcham Congregational Church. Later that year a handsome oak case was presented to the church by Lieut G Franzer, US Army, for the notice board previously presented. The case and board were fixed at the corner of Church Lane, eastern side near the High Street.

By September 1944 an electric organ blower had at long last been installed. Wilfred B Street gave the electric motor and Messrs A H Brown and C G Brown installed the blower.

THE WAR IN EUROPE IS OVER

On Tuesday, 8th May 1945, a large congregation attended the evening thanksgiving service for the end of the war in Europe. The following day a united open air Thanksgiving Service was held in Crown Meadow. It was organized by Revd Owen, the Vicar, the curate, three US Army Chaplains (Capts Cobb, Gereche and McGregor) and a Methodist lay preacher (Mr W Hall). Thatcham Silver Band accompanied the singing.

In June 1945, an application to have alcoholic drinks at a wedding reception in the British School was received. The secretary explained that no intoxicating liquor was allowed on the premises and that the deacons could not depart from this rule.

On 5th November 1946, Henry J Robbins was appointed as organist to succeed the late Godfrey Lay, who died on 10th July 1946. Mr Lay had been church organist since 1917. There is a memorial plaque to Godfrey affixed to the piano currently in use (2005) in the church. Also mentioned on the plaque is William Golding Lay (brother of Godfrey), who died 28th January 1947.

The membership roll at the end of 1946 stood at 138. During the year eight new members had joined, two had died, one transferred out and one resigned, leaving 142 at end of 1947.

On 21st February 1947 Winston Reed was welcomed to the diaconate as a deacon. Other deacons present at this meeting were Mrs Florence Robbins, Miss Mary Jane Pike, Albert Digweed, John H Pike, Edmund Pinnock (junior), A B Vincent Brown (treasurer) and Alfred Robert Brown (secretary).

Mrs Esther (Hettie) Reynolds died in May 1947, aged seventy-five. She was the first lady deacon of our church and served for twenty-nine years. Previously known as Miss Hettie Peters, she married Frederick John Reynolds, a widower, in 1931.

In October 1948, Mr & Mrs George and Morwen Fisher became members on transfer from the Welsh Congregational Church at Brynamman, Carmarthenshire.

In November 1948 a proposal for Congregational-Presbyterian Union was discussed by members. Mrs Pike moved that the "proposed union be given full approval without reserve" but there was no seconder. Then Edmund Pinnock proposed "total dissent" but there was no seconder for that either. After further discussion, members decided without dissent (3 members abstained) - against union with the Presbyterian Church but would welcome a start to negotiations for a union of all the Free Churches.

MEMBERSHIP TOPS 150

Members on roll at the end of 1947 numbered 142. During the year ten new members joined and two lapsed, leaving 150 at end of 1948.

In July 1949 Revd Owen requested an increase in his stipend but owing to the state of the church finances, the matter was deferred for six months.

In January 1950, Revd Owen, having served seven years here, was offered another term. He decided however "to seek a new sphere of service during the next year". He said that "it may be an advantage for the church to have a change of ministry". He had decided to improve himself financially for the sake of his family.

INTOXICATING LIQUOR AND SUNDAY GAMES

In May 1950, Mr E Pinnock moved that "The restriction on intoxicating liquor in the British School be removed". After Revd Owen reported that the deacons were unanimously against this proposal, it was defeated "by a unanimous vote". Also at that meeting, on the matter of Sunday games on the Memorial Playing Field, members agreed unanimously that the church representative "be instructed to oppose any form of Sunday games on the playing fields".

It was reported on 4th July 1950 that Revd Owen had accepted a call to St Clement's Church, Ipswich and would leave Thatcham at the end of August. He preached his farewell sermon at the evening service on Sunday 27th August. After the service a farewell party was held in the British School. Revd Owen was presented with a cheque by Mr J H Pike (senior deacon) and a set of oak tables was presented to Mrs Owen by Mrs Pike. Menna and Eryl Owen received book tokens from Miss Marjorie Brown. Both girls attended Newbury High School in Buckingham Road. Writing from her new school at Ipswich in 1952, Eryl informed the editor of *The Record* (Newbury High School's magazine) that she planned "to follow Menna's example and go to a Teacher Training College in 1954". Menna was then at St Osyth's College, Clacton, Essex.

In July 1950 concern was expressed about the outside lavatory being "used by the general public and left in a very bad state". It was agreed to arrange for the lavatory to be kept locked outside school hours.

In August 1950 it was agreed to purchase 2 & 3 Church Lane for the sum of £750 as a caretaker's house. Number 2 Church Lane was eventually occupied by Norman and Lena Preston (caretakers), while 3 Church Lane was let to Mr & Mrs Aubrey Cass.

Robert Cochrane and Denise Brown at their wedding on 3rd March 1951.
Picture - courtesy of Denise Cochrane.

REVD ROY BOOTH (1951-1962)

Having 'preached with a view' at Thatcham in late 1950, Revd Booth, previously at Bedminster, Bristol, accepted the invitation to become the minister here in January 1951. Roy and Joyce Booth and their two young daughters, Helen and Rosamund, had moved into *The Manse* (69 Bath Road) by April 1951. Revd Booth's induction took place on Wednesday, 16th May 1951. The service was preceded by a tea, attended by about 120 members and friends, including some from Revd Booth's former church at Bedminster.

On 18th August 1951, John Eggleton (one of our current members) was married in our church to Margaret Smith by Revd Booth.

On 9th September 1951, the following were received into church membership - Mr & Mrs Colin Oates, Mrs Gladys Panting and her son Graeme Panting.

In September 1951 Winston Reed reported that intoxicating liquor had been brought into the British School on the occasion of a recent wedding reception. This was noted with considerable concern and appropriate action was to be taken to prevent a recurrence.

On 4th November 1951 a sportsmen's service was held at 6 pm, when members of the Thatcham Cricket Club, Football Club, Badminton Club and Bowls Club attended. Representatives of the clubs took part in the service. Revd Booth gave the address.

In December 1951 members agreed that Revd Booth would oversee the Bucklebury Congregational Church. Woolhampton Congregational Church was already linked in this way to Thatcham Congregational Church. The minister's stipend for the three churches was agreed at £400 per annum.

DEATH OF GEORGE VI, 6th FEBRUARY 1952

A special service in memory of George VI was held on Sunday, 17th February 1952. Revd Booth spoke of the late King's life of service and devotion to duty.

Annual General Meeting, March 1952 - members on the church roll numbered 144 (including twenty associate members) at the end of 1951. There were 102 children and twelve teachers on the Sunday School register (an increase of thirty-five and four respectively over the year).

150th ANNIVERSARY

It was decided in June and July 1952 to open a fund to celebrate 150 years of the opening of our church. Proceeds of the fund would be used to carry out repairs both to the church and the British School and also to redecorate the church. Target for the fund was £1,000. A rally was to be held in January 1954 and a special event was planned for each month during that year. The Women's Own, Social Circle, Choir, Youth Guild and Sunday School were all to be asked to arrange one of the events. There would also be a special concert and a summer fête. The 150th Anniversary Service was arranged for Wednesday, 6th October 1954, when the Moderator, Revd John Phillips, would preside.

On Sunday, 16th November 1952, Miss Heather Churchill was received into church membership.

On Friday, 20th February 1953 Mrs Florence Brown (widow of Arthur Brown and daughter of Robert Vincent) died at her home, aged eighty-one. She had been a life deacon since 1931.

Miss Pearl Cass, Miss Hazel Churchill and Miss Pat Workman were received into church membership at the communion service on Sunday evening, 1st March 1953.

Congregational Church Deacons, 1953.
Back Row: Albert Digweed, Winston Reed, Henry J Robbins, A B Vincent Brown, Alfred Robert Brown, John (Jack) Morris,
Front Row: Mrs Grace Fuller, John H Pike, Revd Roy Booth, Mrs Florence Robbins, Miss Mary Jane Pike.
This picture appeared in the booklet produced for the 150th Anniversary of the Church.

Barbara Gough, one of our current members, was married in our church to Arthur Smith on 18th April 1953 by Revd Booth.

CIVIC SERVICE HELD IN OUR CHURCH

On Sunday, 14th June 1953 Newbury Rural District councillors and Thatcham Parish councillors attended a civic service, taken by Revd Booth at 11 am. This service was held at the invitation of our secretary, Mr A Robert Brown, who was then the chairman of the Newbury Rural District Council.

In October 1953 members agreed to buy a strip of land on the east of the church for £20 and a ten foot-strip on the north for £5 from Ushers Brewery, plus legal expenses.

JUBILEE FETE OPENED BY ARCHERS ACTOR

The Summer Fête, organized by the Social Circle, took place on Saturday 3rd July at *The Priory* by kind permission of Mr and Mrs Montagu Wellby. It was opened by Basil Jones, who played John Tregorran in the BBC radio serial *The Archers*. Despite a rainy start, the fête was a great success and raised £186. This brought the total in the Triple Jubilee Fund to over £800.

In November 1954 Winston Reed, having recently moved from Thatcham to Newbury, announced his resignation from the diaconate. He continued as superintendent of the Sunday School until September 1955.

In 1958 it was decided to sell *Woodlawn* (39 Bath Road), bought as *The Manse* (but never used as such) in 1934 and retained when 69 Bath Road was purchased in 1943 for Revd Owen. It was also decided to sell *The Manse* (69 Bath Road) and purchase a newly built house.

As at 21st October 1958 *Woodlawn* (39 Bath Road) was "virtually sold". It appears to have been sold to the sitting tenants: Albert and Lilian Josling.

It was in January 1959 that the 1st Thatcham Boys' Brigade was founded by Walter Brisk, Arthur Smith and Peter Digweed. Its headquarters have been in the British School ever since that date. Walter Brisk was also the church choirmaster for about two years (1959-61).

By 21st April 1959 the sale of 69 Bath Road was nearing completion. Good progress was also being made on *The (new) Manse*, expected to be ready by June.

NEW ACCOMMODATION FOR PRIMARY DEPARTMENT

It was noted in February 1961 that additional primary accommodation was soon to be provided. Having inspected a steel farmed hut 32 ft 6 ins by 21 ft 5 ins, Mr Aubrey Cass and Mr A Robert Brown reported that the price quoted with 7 ft 6 ins ceiling was £180 erected, plus foundations. It was agreed to seek planning permission for the erection of one of these huts with 8 ft 6 ins ceiling. By May that year a hut had been erected. The installation of heating and lighting "was nearly complete" by 24th October 1961.

Mrs L Morwen Fisher replaced Mr A Robert Brown as church secretary at the start of 1962.

Revd Booth preached his last sermon at Thatcham Congregational Church on 13th May 1962. He left Thatcham for Leek, Staffordshire, on 17th May after eleven years ministry in Thatcham.

REVD FREDERICK SPRIGGS (1962-1973)

Revd Spriggs 'preached with a view' in our church on 17th June 1962. All the deacons were favourably impressed by his approach. He visited again in July with his wife Rosemary, preaching at Bucklebury in the morning, Woolhampton in the afternoon and at Thatcham in the evening, with light refreshments in the British School after the evening service. In that same month members accepted the unanimous recommendation of the deacons that Frederick Spriggs be invited to become our minister. Fred and Rosemary with their daughter Karin and son Andrew moved into *The (new) Manse*, 26 Beverley Close, on 10th September 1962. Revd Spriggs, who was previously at Speke Congregational Church, Liverpool, began his ministry here on Sunday 16th September. There was no time limit (previously five years) placed on the duration of his ministry. His induction as minister took place on 28th September 1962.

Fred was born 30th March 1919 at Greetham near Qakham in Rutland. He grew up in that county and upon leaving school at fourteen years of age, he went to work in the laboratory of a cement company at Ketton. After a few years there, he decided that he would like to be a Congregational Church minister and duly enrolled for training at Payton College, Nottingham.

The Second World War interrupted that training. Being a man of peace and a conscientious objector, Fred spent the next six years working on the land. After the war he returned to the college to finish his training and was ordained on 29th July 1948 at the Congregational Church in Painswick, Gloucestershire. Earlier that same month Fred had married Rosemary Smith at Theddingworth, Leicestershire. They had first met there at the Congregational Church, where Fred used to preach as a student just after the war.

Fred and Rosemary lived at Painswick for four years. Their son Andrew was born there. In 1952 they moved to Buckingham, where Fred was inducted as the Congregational minister. It was while they were living in Buckingham that their daughter Karin was born and Fred served as chaplain to the Mayor of Buckingham during the latter's term of office. In 1959 the family moved to Speke, Liverpool, where Fred continued his ministry during a stay of three years.

In October 1962, Mrs Rosemary Spriggs offered to form a junior choir; Mr Llyn Jones expressed a wish to form a drama group and Mrs White offered to embroider a cloth for the communion table - all were accepted with thanks by members.

FAREWELL OLD TOILET BLOCK

In November 1962 the old toilet block in the playground of the British School was being demolished by voluntary workers but "there was still a lot more (work) to do" said Mr A B V Brown. A firm in Newbury had agreed to cart away the bricks without charge.

In January 1963 the church membership stood at 137 (including twenty-three associate members), there having been four new members, three who died, two lapsed and two transferred in during 1962. Officers elected: treasurer A B Vincent Brown; secretary Mrs L M Fisher; supply secretary Mrs Ann Sellwood.

In February 1963 Peter Digweed resigned as Captain of the Boys' Brigade but continued for a while as a lieutenant. Arthur Smith was appointed as captain, with Lionel Sandy remaining as a lieutenant.

Also in February 1963, a complaint was received about the Junior Church bus, which carried the children to church on Sunday mornings - it was causing a nuisance to the residents when parked in Church Lane. The secretary was asked to write to the Thames Valley Bus Company requesting that the bus park either in High Street or in the Broadway.

CHRISTIAN AID COMMITTEE FORMED

It was in 1963 that the United Nations Freedom from Hunger Campaign was launched. On 6th April that year a bread and cheese lunch, organized by Graeme Panting in the parlour, raised £6-10-0 for that campaign. There followed the inauguration of the Christian Aid Week. The local initiative for this arose at the

Thatcham Ministers Fraternal, an ecumenical group of the clergy in Thatcham. The driving force behind the initiative was our minister, Frederick Spriggs. A Christian Aid Committee was formed and Fred was appointed as its first secretary. The first collection envelopes were distributed to collectors on 7th May 1963. In that first year the house-to-house collection plus the use of a Christian Aid shop in the High Street resulted in the sum of £254 being raised during the week.

OFFICERS ELECTED 1964

Revd Spriggs and thirty-eight members were present at the AGM on 14th January 1964. Officers elected were - church treasurer A B Vincent Brown, church secretary Mrs L Morwen Fisher, organist & choirmaster Henry J Robbins, choir secretary Miss Iris Matthews, Junior Department leader Mrs Hilda Flitter, Primary Department leader Miss Susan Colbourne; London Missionary Society secretary Mrs Mary Sugden; Women's Own leader Mrs Alice Digweed, secretary Mrs Phyllis Read; Social Circle convenor & treasurer Mrs Gwen Eggleton; Friendship Club leader Mrs L M Fisher, acting secretary Mrs K Kilberry, treasurer Mrs Rosemary Spriggs; Sports Club secretary Graeme Panting; duplicator secretary Mrs Denise Cochrane; The Link treasurer Miss Jill Langdon; Temperance Society representative Graeme Panting.

At the church meeting on 28th April 1964 in the parlour (thirty-one present), "there was a lively and interesting discussion on the Christian attitude towards the consumption of alcoholic drinks, particularly amongst young people". This arose from a letter received from "prominent Congregationalists", who expressed concern on the matter.

In May 1964 Mrs Hilda Flitter resigned as leader of the Junior Department and Mrs Amy Hale was appointed in her place.

In September 1964 the following appointments to the staff of the Junior Church were confirmed - Miss Georgina Slade and Roy Tubb.

Postcard picture of Thatcham High Street taken about 1960. This postcard was signed by fourteen children from the Junior Church (Anthony Amor, John Berntsen, Keith Buckell, David Eggleton, David Harris, Stephen Parfitt, David Risley, Edward Risley, Stephen Risley, Christine Sloan, Kathryn Sloan, Andrew Spriggs, Graham Toms, John Walters) and posted to the author of this book, who was working in USA at the time (1965-66).

NOT A SUITABLE NAME

In November 1964 the deacons considered that 'The Hut' was not a suitable name for the new building and recommended that in future it should be called 'The Primary Room'. The railings at the front of the British School would, in the interest of safety, be removed completely within the next three weeks.

In September 1965 - "With a feeling of real gratitude", the church meeting endorsed the appointment of six new teachers in the Junior Church. The appointments were as follows: Primary Department - Miss Pauline Rogers, Mrs Irene Barr, Mrs Stella Hutchings, Andrew Spriggs: Junior Department - Peter Jones and Mrs Violet Tubb. The Senior Group continued with Miss Iris Matthews and Arthur Smith.

In November 1965 it was planned to restart a Youth Club (last run by David and Gill Humphrey) on Friday 17th December next. Hilary Wheeler, Robin Wheeler and Malcolm Davies would act as leaders. By the end of January 1966 the Youth Club had been going satisfactorily for several weeks with twenty to twenty-five youngsters attending.

Church treasurer A B Vincent Brown retired after thirty-five years in January 1966 and was replaced by David Jeffery Martin.

On 1st March 1966 members held a special church meeting to discuss some of the implications of the preliminary talks on the possible union of the Congregational Church in England and Wales and the Presbyterian Church of England.

MORALITY UNDER DISCUSSION

In October 1966 a conference, attended by Revd Spriggs and fourteen members, was held in the Primary Room. Members discussed a report recently produced by the British Council of Churches on 'sex and morality'. Relevant points made included "the increase in venereal diseases and illegitimacy" and the fact that young people were being exposed to "manifestations of immorality through the media of television, radio and questionable literature".

EXPENSE OF THE CHURCH BUS

In June 1967 concern was expressed about the cost of the church bus. It was running at a loss to the church, being used by only 20-25 people, including some Methodists. If the bus were cancelled it was thought that some of our children might not come to church. Two years later (July 1969), increased fares were agreed - from Southdown Road 1/- per adult, 6d per child and from the top of Park Lane 6d per adult, 3d per child (all return fares). Two months later a further increase in the fare from the top of Park Lane was necessary - adults would have to pay 8d and children 4d each. By November 1971 the number of passengers using the bus had dwindled to a maximum of about four children and ten adults, so it was decided to discontinue the service from 19th December 1971.

On Saturday 15th July 1967 the junior church picnic was held at Mr Andrew Nesbit's Malthouse Farm at Beenham and a great time was enjoyed by all who shared the day. There were over sixty children and about thirty adults altogether. Several adults joined in the fun, which included rounders, a treasure hunt, non-stop cricket, races and football. Revd Spriggs, having just injured himself in a fall on the road, was unable to go this year.

At the AGM on 9th January 1968, deacons were re-elected as follows - Mrs L Morwen Fisher, Arnold Aubrey and Norman Chapman (all unopposed). Mrs Hughes was elected (also unopposed) to take the place of Mrs Ann Sellwood.

At a church meeting on 26th November 1968, it was pointed out that when the Girls' Brigade Company joins the parade, the young people almost fill the whole of the church downstairs. For these occasions it was suggested that the Primary Department should meet in its own room.

CONGO CRICKET CLUB

In June 1969 Graeme Panting wrote to the deacons stating that the Congregational Cricket Club wished to use the name 'Congo' in place of the name of 'Congregational'. He also asked permission to use the British School for serving teas and suggested 5/- for each occasion. Both of his suggestions met with disapproval from the deacons. It transpired however, that the name Thatcham Congo Cricket Club was eventually adopted and the club continued to play under that name until about 2002, when the club ceased playing cricket.

PILOTS COMING TO THATCHAM

On 7th October 1969 Revd Spriggs reported that because of the decrease in the membership of Bucklebury Pilots, it would be easier to transport the children from Bucklebury and meet here in Thatcham. Members agreed with this suggestion. Reports on other organizations were also given at that meeting: these included one from the Social Circle - "the senior organization, having been meeting for about sixty years and formerly known as the Sewing Meeting". Its object was to make and sell goods to raise funds for repair of church buildings. It had a membership of eighteen in 1969. A report on the Women's Own mentioned that it was founded in 1924 and always aimed to have a varied programme of meetings. Its members also took their part in the Women's Auxiliary of the County Union.

Another report described the Friendship Club which had been meeting for ten years. Its membership had remained static and had "little appeal because the meetings were held on church premises". Competition had recently arisen with the formation of a branch of the Townswomen's Guild in Thatcham.

Also at that meeting, it was suggested that grown-ups sit with the children during the morning services "in an effort to maintain order and quietness before and during the service".

Old newspapers were being collected at the church in 1969 - Miller's of Newbury had agreed to collect the old newspapers when a sufficient quantity was accumulated at the church.

At the church meeting on 13th January 1970, Revd Spriggs and thirty-six members were present. The following appointments were confirmed - Junior Department leader Jill Wilson, Primary Department leader Rosemary Spriggs, Girls' Brigade Captain Doreen Pickersgill, Lieutenants Mrs Beatrice Chapman and Miss Beryl Chapman, Boys' Brigade Captain Arthur Smith, Lieutenants Dennis Perris, George Pickersgill and Norman Chapman.

CONGREGATIONAL-METHODIST UNION DISCUSSED

On 28th April 1970 Sister Daphne with other leaders and trustees of the Methodist Church met Revd Spriggs and the deacons of the Congregational Church in Thatcham to discuss a union of the two churches. It was unanimously agreed at that meeting "to proceed with further investigation". These talks arose following the refusal of a planning application for enlargement of the Methodist Church premises. The Minister of Transport had objected on highway grounds. However, the minister subsequently agreed not to object to an amended plan and the talks on a scheme of union between the two churches were terminated. Nevertheless, all concerned agreed that they had been "of great value" and regular united services with the Methodists were to be held.

In July 1970 membership of the Girls' Brigade stood at fifty-one, an increase of ten over last year. The Pilots, run by Revd Spriggs, had a membership of fifteen at that time.

CONGREGATIONAL - PRESBYTERIAN UNION

By 24th November 1970 the final draft for the proposed Congregational - Presbyterian Scheme of Union had been published. At the 1971 Assembly, a vote would be taken whether to proceed - 75% of those present and voting would be needed. It would then go to County Unions and if approved, to local churches for them to vote by December 1971.

A special church meeting was held on Tuesday 26th October 1971 to discuss the proposed scheme of union between the Congregational Church in England and Wales and the Presbyterian Church of England. Present were eleven members from Bucklebury Congregational Church, one from Woolhampton Congregational Church and sixty-nine from Thatcham Congregational Church. After discussion at Thatcham, members voted by ballot, the results being Thatcham 66-3 in favour. Bucklebury, on the other hand, voted 6-5 against and remained outside the union. The County Union had already voted 124-12 in favour. The actual union took place at a United Assembly on 5th October 1972.

WOOLHAMPTON CHURCH IN TROUBLE

In February 1971 Woolhampton Congregational Church was closed for services because the cost of immediate repairs (£400 - £500) could not be met. Until such time as the money could be found, services were to be held in the Gill Campbell Memorial Hall from 28th March. In July of that same year it was decided that the church building be closed for good and the site sold. The trust deed required that the church had to remain closed for eighteen months before it could be sold. The organ and chinaware were to be transferred to the Gill Campbell Hall. By November 1971 the Woolhampton finances had been merged with those of Thatcham.

A MEMBER FOR SEVENTY-THREE YEARS

At the Annual General Church Meeting on 16th January 1973, with thirty-two present, before proceeding with the business, members stood in remembrance of Mrs Violet Tubb and Mrs M Wooldridge, who had died since the last meeting. At the church meeting on 27th March 1973 members stood in remembrance of Mrs Tiffen, who had died since the last church meeting. On 29th May 1973 members stood in memory of Mrs A H Brown who had recently died, aged ninety-six: she became a member in 1900 and in her earlier days had taken a very active part in the church and the village.

DEATH OF REVD SPRIGGS

In February 1973 Revd Spriggs was unwell and had to see a specialist. Mrs Spriggs asked to be relieved for the time being of her duties in the Junior Church, Women's Own and Junior Choir. Appointed in her place were Mrs Joyce Marshall and Miss Glynis Fisher in the Primary Department and Mrs Hughes in the Women's Own. Mrs Irvine agreed to continue her work with the junior choir for the time being. The silver wedding anniversary of Frederick and Rosemary Spriggs occurred on 10th July 1973 but by that time Fred was seriously ill. He died in Newbury Hospital, Andover Road, on 28th August that same year. Cremation took place at Oxford after which a memorial service at the URC in Thatcham was attended by about four hundred people. Rosemary remained in Thatcham, a staunch member of our church until 2nd December 2004, when she moved to Cheshire to be nearer her daughter Karin, who is married with two children, Helen and David. Andrew Spriggs, who became a teacher, tragically drowned in a swimming pool in 1982, aged thirty-one.

Fred was a kind, patient and understanding pastor. He went about his work in a quiet and friendly way. He loved being with and helping children and this found expression in his work with 'Pilots', a national young people's church organization with emphasis on world mission. Fred was the national organizer; he wrote material for Pilot log books and organized camping expeditions. For five years he served as a Pilot Officer until shortly before his death. He also wrote Bible study material and Christmas stories for children; he worked very closely with the Junior Church leaders in the congregation at Thatcham.

In the words of Revd Colin Richards of Newbury, Frederick Spriggs had a "depth of perception" and a "clarity of expression" which was known not only by his congregations but to many people outside the various churches in which he preached. He served as a governor of Kennet School for several years. He was an energetic advocate of world mission and action against world poverty, contributing much to the initiation of Christian Aid in Thatcham, for which he tirelessly worked and walked. A leading role was played by him in the Newbury District Council of Churches, of which he was chairman in 1971-72. Service to the administration of his own denomination is evidenced by his time as secretary of the Congregational Central District Council and in 1970 by his being elected chairman of the Berks, South Oxon and South Bucks Congregational Union. Spriggs Close, Thatcham, is named after Fred Spriggs.

KENNET VALLEY SCHEME SCUPPERED BY THATCHAM

At a meeting on 30th October 1973, with forty-seven present and Revd Colin Richards of Newbury presiding, the Kennet Valley Churches Scheme was discussed. This would have seen all the United Reformed Churches in the Kennet Valley loosely linked together and co-operating in as many ways as possible. Mrs Beatrice Chapman and Mrs Janice Baldwin spoke in favour of the scheme in principle and others spoke firmly in favour. Some members saw no advantage whatsoever and wished to be assured that a minister would be based in Thatcham. A vote showed twenty-one to be in favour and twenty-five against: one member abstained. Following this decision, Mrs Geary (secretary of Newbury URC) spoke of "that church's disappointment at the fall-down of the scheme. They had looked forward to sharing fellowship with the churches in the group." It appears that Thatcham scuppered the whole scheme.

During the Christmas period of 1973, Revd Raymond Coke of Jamaica served as acting minister of our church for about three weeks. During his stay here he lodged with Mary and Alan Cooper at *Old Henwick Cottage*.

REVD ARTHUR BAKER (1974-1989)

On 27th January 1974 Revd Arthur Baker 'preached with a view', preaching morning and evening. He was accompanied by his wife June and their children Andrew, Rowena and Gwyneth. Arthur was subsequently invited by members to become the minister of Thatcham United Reformed Church. The family moved to Thatcham in April from Chandlers Ford (Hampshire) but Arthur did not conduct any services until after his induction service, which took place on Tuesday 21st May 1974.

Arthur Baker was born in Glamorgan and spent his boyhood in Mountain Ash, on the Afon Cynon. He joined the Royal Air Force in 1941 as a fifteen-year-old apprentice, stationed at first in Oxfordshire. Arthur qualified as an airframe fitter and travelled the world, courtesy of the RAF. He spent his nineteenth birthday in India, his twentieth in Australia and his twenty-first in Italy. He left the RAF in 1948 and after a brief stay at an aeronautical college, he took a succession of jobs in engineering. In 1952 he enrolled at Rawdon College, near Bradford (West Riding of Yorkshire) and was ordained as a Baptist minister in 1956. It was at Rawdon that Arthur met June: they were married in 1957 at Guiseley, West Riding. Arthur's first church as minister was at Wallsend, Northumberland, where he remained until 1960. He then moved to Shropshire, where he was minister concurrently for two churches, one at Madeley, the other at Broseley. In 1964 Arthur joined the Langley House Trust, a national charity for the welfare of ex-prisoners. June and Arthur worked as house parents in charge of a hostel for former prisoners. After ten years in that work, Arthur decided to return to the priesthood, "a very much more down-to-earth person" than when he had left it.

Mrs June Baker, an organist and a piano teacher before she came to Thatcham, was fully supportive of Arthur in the church. She concentrated on youth work in Thatcham. She did this very successfully. It was June who inaugurated the weekly coffee morning in the British School, which has continued each Tuesday morning to the present time. She also developed her talent as an opera singer in Newbury.

At the AGM in January 1974 Norman Chapman retired after eight years as a deacon and elder. He was replaced by Miss Iris Matthews. The other serving elders at this time were - Mrs Janice Baldwin, Mrs Margaret Bowen, Mrs Beatrice Chapman, Mrs Gwen Eggleton, Mrs L Morwen Fisher, Dennis Gill, Mrs Amy Hale, Eric Hughes, Graeme Panting and Arthur Smith.

GIRLS' BRIGADE DISBANDED

The Girls' Brigade (started in 1967-68) was disbanded early in 1974. This decision, made very reluctantly, followed a period of temporary closure owing to power cuts that resulted from the national miners' strike that year. Numbers had declined. There were also staff shortages - Mrs Doreen Pickersgill (the captain) had taken on extra work in the political field and was unable to devote as much time to the Girls' Brigade and Beryl Chapman was about to move away from this area. Mrs Beatrice Chapman was also somewhat uncertain about her future place of residence at that time.

As at March 1974 'The Link' magazine (newsletter) was being printed by Mrs Geary and her daughter of Newbury URC. Because the cost to them was to increase from £3·50 to £5 per month, members agreed to pay an extra 10p each per year (up from 15p to 25p per year).

Mr and Mrs Arnold Aubrey moved from Thatcham to Shrewsbury in March 1974.

In September 1974 Mrs Baker reported on the success of the newly formed youth group, the One Way Club, which she had recently started. Twenty-four youngsters attended the first meeting.

As at January 1975 there were four organists available for services - Henry Robbins, Miss Iris Matthews, Mrs Barbara Ford and Mrs June Baker.

In March 1975, June Baker reported that the church choir numbered about fourteen. Opportunity had been taken to join with choirs from Brimpton, Bucklebury and St Mary's, Thatcham. It was planned to present The Passion of Christ at Easter next. Iris Matthews reported on the junior section of the Boys' Brigade, which had taken part in church parades, a basketball competition, go-kart racing and six-a-side football. About fourteen boys attended summer camp at Southsea. There were about twenty junior boys on roll at that time.

CHURCH TO BE KEPT LOCKED

In July 1975 members discussed the security of the church premises. The elders had recommended that the church be kept locked, it being a necessary step "owing to the increased vandalism in Thatcham". Whilst not meeting with everybody's approval, the recommendation was accepted by a majority. Revd Baker offered to be at the church at an arranged time in order for people to see the church or use it for prayer.

In November 1975 members voted 12-5 with 8 abstentions to move the Sunday evening service to 3 pm during December, January and February.

In January 1976 Norman and Beatrice Chapman had their membership transferred to Newbury URC. In February that year Frank and Barbara Howlett were received into membership at Thatcham.

WOOLHAMPTON SERVICES TO CEASE

Church services at Woolhampton had been held in the Gill Campbell Hall from March 1971, when the church building was closed. After the last Sunday in November 1976 church services at Woolhampton ceased. This decision was taken after careful consideration of the following facts - Mr Strutt had taken on more work at Brimpton Baptist Church, where both he and his wife were members; Mr and Mrs Purdy had requested membership at Thatcham; Mrs

Oakes had been attending the Church of England at Woolhampton, which left just one other member of the URC at Woolhampton.

The United Reformed Church building at Woolhampton was sold by auction on 24th May 1973 for £2,175 to Mr Wastie of Warner's Bakery nearby. It was eventually demolished and replaced in about 1978 by a dwelling-house named *Rum Hole*.

In 1976 it was decided to enlarge the church vestibule by removing about two rows of pews and moving the screen eastward. However, a structural engineer's report that the screen was bearing some of the weight of the balcony and the consequent extra cost persuaded members to abandon the scheme at that time. Twenty-seven years later another surveyor's report revealed that the screen was not bearing any weight of the balcony.

Rowena Baker and John Hutchings left Thatcham in 1977, Rowena to take up a nursing career and John to attend teacher training college. They were both teachers in the Primary Department. Leader of that department, Joyce Marshall, expressed thanks for their hard work and devotion to the children.

Mrs Amy Hale, the church secretary, announced in 1977 that she had decided to move near to her family in the Forest of Dean area and would therefore have to resign as secretary in the near future. Revd Arthur Baker paid tribute to Amy's excellent work over the past years. Mrs Mary Gray was appointed in her place. The Busy Bees Playgroup, which had been using the Primary Room nearly every weekday for ten years, ceased using the premises on 2nd June 1978. The group was established in 1968 by church member Doreen Pickersgill, who served as chairman of its management committee for about five years.

RAFFLES & GAMES OF CHANCE NOT POPULAR

In June 1978, members were discussing fund raising when Julian Spence proposed that "raffles and games of chance" were a valid and acceptable means of raising money for the church. He did not consider these to be gambling. He was supported by Alan Cooper and Revd Baker, the latter pointing out that "there was nothing in the Bible against lotteries and games of chance". The discussion which followed revealed that "deep feelings against games of chance" were held by many members, while others thought that "raffles and milder forms of lotteries" were acceptable. Because this was "such an emotive subject" with members about equally divided, no firm decision was made, except that by implication the church would not be organizing any raffles in the near future.

Church and British School renovation work, which included essential repairs to the church roof, was carried out in 1978-79 by H A Stradling & Sons Ltd for £8,500.

CHURCH MEETINGS NOT WELL ATTENDED
On 24th October 1978, members were concerned about poor attendance at church meetings. There were about twenty present at this meeting but "in general attendances had fallen very low". There were only nine members in attendance at the previous month's meeting. It was noted however that when important items were announced in advance, much larger attendances were realized. In order to improve the situation, members voted 14-0 to hold church meetings just once every quarter. Furthermore, it was decided to publish the agenda well in advance and to concentrate on church policy at the meetings rather than on church administration which could be left to the elders. Finally, Bible study groups to take place in private houses would be arranged throughout the year.

In January 1979 Eric Hughes (an elder) announced that he and his wife, Eva, would shortly be leaving Thatcham for Lichfield, Staffordshire. Another elder, Margaret Fidler, said she would like to stand down for a year. Three new elders were elected - David Gray, Mary Cooper and Graeme Panting.

At the AGM on 22nd January 1980, Arthur Smith stepped down from the eldership. Mrs L Morwen Fisher and Miss Iris Matthews were re-elected to continue for another term. Mrs Margaret Fidler was elected after her break of one year and Mrs Trudy Mardell was elected as a new elder.

CIVIC SERVICE WAS WELL ATTENDED

A civic service was held on Sunday, 25th May 1980 at Thatcham URC. Two of our members were then serving on Thatcham Town Council - Roy Tubb (Town Mayor at the time) and George Pickersgill. Other local councillors also attended, including another eight from Thatcham Town Council and some from Cold Ash and Bucklebury Parish Councils.

At the church meeting on Tuesday, 21st October 1980, members stood in silence for two minutes in memory of Henry John Robbins, who had recently died. Henry was our church organist for thirty-four years from 1946.

On 20th January 1981 Revd Baker announced that 1981 would mark the 25th year of his ordination. He spoke of his seven years in Thatcham and of the good work done in those years. He believed that the work of the church was spreading out into the wider community. However, over the preceding two years, he had been aware that all had not been well and "he had felt aware of powers of darkness telling him to go away". He asked for support from all working together for him and June.

ONE WAY CLUB FLOURISHING

In April 1982 June Baker reported on the progress of the One Way Youth Club. Numbers had increased from about nine regulars to about sixteen and those in the handicapped group had grown to about fourteen, which made a total of about thirty each week. Two new assistants had been recruited - Mike Harmsworth of the Green Lane Mission Church joined early in 1981 and later Lou Cummins (editor of the Newbury Weekly News) went in to help. Other helpers were Mary Cooper, Hazel Dempster, Janet Hood and David Gray. Activities during the winter months included indoor games, discussions, refreshments and singing together, while in the summer they had as many outdoor activities as possible.

BOYS' BRIGADE'S MIXED FORTUNES

Also in April 1982 Captain Arthur Smith and Lieutenant Iris Matthews reported on the Boys' Brigade. Regrettably, said Arthur, the number of boys in the Company Section was down from sixteen to eight over the past year: this was due in part, he said, to families leaving the area and some boys joining cadet forces. Arthur was pleased with the bible classes, "the best for many years", thanks largely to Margaret Fidler, who also gave first aid lessons. The band was struggling but still progressing under Mike Huntley. Trevor Quenualt and Peter Digweed had ably assisted in the Company Section. However, Arthur was not hopeful about the Company Section continuing for much longer. He was, on the other hand, optimistic regarding the young Robins (six to eight year old boys) run by Mrs Josie Ayres. There were sixteen boys in that section and most of them also attended Junior Church. The Robins were eventually renamed the Anchor Boys.

The Junior Section report was given by Iris, who said that they had a regular attendance of about twenty boys each week and three lady officers. The annual display evening in May was packed with parents and friends, who witnessed a varied programme performed by boys from all sections. Six boys received the gold badge, the highest award in the junior section. The annual summer camp, attended by about thirty, was at Exmouth in Devon, where the local Boys' Brigade took part in games and shared a party with the Thatcham group. In September the Junior Section, accompanied by 2nd Thatcham Brownies, took part in the Thatcham Carnival as the Black and White Minstrels - they won first prize. They have continued with the usual activities, such as badge work, figure marching, music, group work, games, gymnastics and church parades.

The Company Section did close for a brief period but reopened, when junior boys had attained the required age. Other officers of the Boys' Brigade around that time and afterwards have included - Officer i/c Junior Section Barbara Smith, Officer i/c Junior Section Tess Smith, Rita Pocock, Janet Gilbert, Christine Brazier, Heather Millson, Barry Holdway, David Parsons, Linda Roberts and Anchor Boys' Leader (from January 1994) Ann Robinson. Helpers since 1982 have included Malcolm Langford and Kevin Roberts.

In 1987 David Brazier came to Thatcham Boys' Brigade from Luton and was given the task of reviving the Company Section. In 1999, David was promoted to Captain of the Brigade. At the same time Arthur Smith was made President of Thatcham Boys' Brigade.

SIXTEEN BAPTISMS IN ONE YEAR
Phyllis Read reported that sixteen baptisms had taken place in our church in the year ended 31st March 1982. She added that there were then forty-nine babies on the church cradle roll. Birthday cards were sent to them all until their fourth birthday.

In January 1984 members were informed that our church building had been officially listed by the Department of the Environment as being of historical and architectural importance. In that month Marion Broughton's membership was transferred to Thatcham URC from Watford URC.

Arthur Brudenell Vincent Brown died on 31st May 1984, aged eighty-eight. Vincent Brown (as he was usually known) was a member of our church for seventy-one years and for over half that time (thirty-six years in fact) he served as church treasurer.

In January 1985 members noted the retirement of Mrs Barbara Smith and Miss Iris Matthews from the Boys' Brigade, in which each had served for twenty-six years. Arthur Smith was to continue in command of the Boys' Brigade for one more year in order to train the new officers. The rank of warrant officer was then confirmed on Mrs Tess Smith, Mrs Janet Gilbert, Mrs Rita Pocock and Mrs Heather Millson.

At the church meeting on 24th April 1985, George Pickersgill (in the chair) informed members of the elders' recommendation to borrow £10,000 from the URC Reading & Oxford District to replace the primary room with a brick building. Richard Wallington presented a plan for the new building and after much discussion it was agreed that tenders for construction be sought as soon as possible. The contract was eventually agreed with Pipers (Ashmore Green) Ltd. It was hoped that the new building would be finished by June 1986.

RAFFLES ARE OKAY FOR THE CHURCH

Also on 24th April 1985, members discussed a church meeting resolution of 1959, which prohibited raffles on church premises. The elders' recommendation that it be rescinded was agreed by a majority. Of the twenty members present, four voted against, one of whom expressed "very strong views against this decision".

In July 1985, Iris Matthews reported on the proposed new United Churches Link Magazine. Members wholeheartedly agreed that Thatcham URC should participate in the new Thatcham Link magazine, to start from January 1986. This was to replace the URC Link then in circulation.

Shortly before October 1986, arrangements had been made with Manpower Services to have all the pews and the pulpit-organ woodwork stripped of the dark brown paint. This work was virtually complete by the end of 1987. The pews were stained and finished in clear varnish, while the pulpit-organ woodwork was merely finished in clear varnish. No charge was to be made for labour: the cost of materials was about £600.

In January 1987 Alan Mossman was appointed as church secretary. He succeeded the Revd Arthur Baker, who had served as secretary for nearly five years.

DISTRICT PASTORAL CARE VISITATION

In October 1987 four members of the URC Reading & Oxford District Pastoral Care Committee visited Thatcham. After attending an elders' meeting, a church meeting and two church services, they compiled a report for members to read. They noted that the membership then numbered seventy-two. Sunday morning worship attracted about sixty adults each week. Junior Church comprised three groups (primary, junior and senior) with an average total weekly attendance of about forty-five. A weekly evening service was held jointly with the Anglicans and Methodists but attendances had fallen to a low level and consideration was being given to its discontinuance.

The serving elders as from January 1988 were - Mrs June Baker, Mrs Joan Ball, Mrs Stella Hutchings, Malcolm Langford, Miss Iris Matthews, Alan Mossman, Mrs Doreen Pickersgill, George Pickersgill, Mrs Olive Pulley, Mrs Phyllis Read, Mrs Rosemary Spriggs and Richard Wallington. Mrs Rosemary Spriggs was newly elected in January 1988 to replace Mrs Morwen Fisher, who had recently died.

ARTHUR BAKER TO RETIRE

In December 1988 it was announced that Arthur's last Sunday as minister would be 29th January 1989. An official farewell gathering was arranged for the following March. Arthur and June moved to Catterall near Garstang, Lancashire. Revd Winston Reed, then in retirement and living in Newbury, was appointed Interim Moderator for Thatcham URC, pending the appointment of a new minister.

The church choir appears to have been dissolved when June Baker left. Almost from the moment she arrived in Thatcham, it was June who had kept the choir going.

REVD DAPHNE CELIA WILLIAMS (1989-1993)

In February 1989 Revd Reed advised members that Miss Daphne Williams, a student who had spent the last year at Mansfield College, had been recommended to Thatcham by Revd Nelson Bainbridge (Moderator of Wessex Synod). Miss Williams was duly invited by Thatcham URC to 'preach with a view' here on 9th April. Three days later members met and voted overwhelmingly (33-1) in favour of offering Miss Williams the pastorate. This she gladly accepted. Her ordination at Thatcham took place on Saturday 22nd July 1989 at 3 pm. Representatives of the local Church of England, Roman Catholic, Baptist and Methodist Churches were present at this service along with about sixty regular adherents of the Thatcham United Reformed Church. Revd Bainbridge presided over the service.

Daphne was formerly a secondary school teacher. Born at Burnham, Buckinghamshire, she was baptized in Burnham Congregational Church. Daphne grew up there until she was ten years of age, when she moved to Marlow with her parents. She became a member of the Marlow Congregational Church in 1971. Her mother, Stella Williams, was a local district lay preacher. Daphne attended Wycombe High School, following which she graduated from Nottingham University. After studying for another year, she gained a post-graduate certificate in education. During 1977-80 she taught geography at Ongar Comprehensive School in Chipping Ongar, Essex. Her next appointment was at Price's Sixth Form College, Fareham, Hampshire, where she taught geography and geology until 1985. It was while she was working at Fareham that Daphne's thoughts turned towards a new career. This was triggered during a month-long expedition to Zambia in 1981. Those on the trip, which was organized by the United Reformed Church, were guests of the United Church of Zambia, a Church that was formed from Congregational, Methodist and Presbyterian

Churches. Four years later (1985) Daphne started a four-year church ministry course at Mansfield College, Oxford. During her training period for the ministry she preached at Fulham and Hammersmith United Reformed Churches.

LET'S HAVE MORE CHURCH MEETINGS

In September 1989 the frequency of church meetings was discussed. They were then being held quarterly. Elders' meetings were held monthly. Alan Cooper spoke in favour of increased frequency of church meetings and after discussion, his proposal that henceforth both church and elders' meetings be held bi-monthly in alternate months except August, was agreed by the meeting.

The regular weekly social gatherings in the British School after each Sunday morning service were first suggested by Daphne in January 1990. She said that something she enjoyed in all the churches in which she had trained was coffee after the service, not just on parade days (once a month) but every Sunday.

In March 1990 Mike Payne was elected as another 'authorized person', in addition to Revd Daphne Williams and George Fisher, to act for the Superintendent Registrar in the registration of weddings at the church.

On Easter Sunday 1990 Arthur and Barbara Smith prepared and served a cooked breakfast on church premises - "the fellowship was a great success". The Easter Day breakfasts have continued to the present time (2005) and have been cooked and served by Sandra and John Baron since about 1997.

In May of 1990 David Weller was received into church membership and Kevin Roberts likewise in June.

THE PAGAN FESTIVAL OF HALLOWEEN

In July 1990 it was reported to members that all the clergy in Thatcham were concerned about the pagan celebration of Halloween. They were particularly disturbed that schools and youth clubs might be enthusing children about Halloween and had contacted all schools and youth groups in an attempt to discourage such celebrations. An "Alternative to Halloween Party" was arranged at the Roman Catholic Church Hall on 31st October that year.

In September 1990 members resolved to transfer the trusteeship of the building of the Thatcham URC from the United Reformed Church Trust to the United Reformed Church (Wessex) Trust Ltd.

Mrs Gwen Eggleton died on 7th November 1990, aged eighty-eight. She was a church member for many years and joined the choir in the 1920s. Gwen (née Chandler) married Stanley Eggleton in our church in 1926. Stanley also sang in the choir. There is a plaque in the entrance porch of the British School which refers to the cast iron gates at the front of the porch. The gates were erected in memory of Gwen. She actually attended the British School as a child and was transferred to the Council School (Francis Baily School) when the British School closed in 1913.

In July 1991 Sandra and John Baron were received into church membership.

VISIONS OF REVD WILLIAMS AND ALAN COOPER

In September 1991 Revd Williams told members of a vision she had experienced of "a new church in the middle of a growing community, being part of an ecumenical setting". Alan Cooper reported a similar vision he had experienced. Some members were cautious and raised questions about the future of our church buildings in Church Lane. The general attitude was that careful thought would be needed by all concerned in such an important matter. After a lengthy discussion in the following November it became evident that of the five main denominations in Thatcham, only the Anglicans had shown any interest in a newly built ecumenical church and many of our own members wished to retain our own church, situated as it is in the town centre. Nevertheless, Revd Williams was advised to "keep talking" to others about the proposition. It was reported in January 1993 that very little progress on this project had been made but it did appear that as well as the Church of England, the Baptist Church was interested. By March however that interest had evaporated and "the likelihood of a church being built on Dunston Park in the foreseeable future was extremely remote". However, a Declaration of Intent was signed on 6th June 1993 at an open air service in the field where the Community Hall was going to be built.

PROTEST ABOUT SUNDAY TRADING

In November 1991 Mike Payne urged members to write to the local MP to register their disapproval of the proposed relaxation of the restrictions on Sunday shop opening hours. Parliament was soon to abolish most of the restrictions and all shops were allowed to remain open for six hours on Sundays.

Also in that November Alan Cooper resigned as church secretary, owing to the fact that he and his wife Mary had just moved to Shalbourne, Wiltshire. They had been connected with our church for twenty years. Alan was replaced by John Baron, who served in that post until May 1992, when David Weller was appointed as secretary.

It was also agreed in November 1991 to discontinue The Link magazine which was "no longer fulfilling its need as an ecumenical magazine". Members decided to produce a Thatcham URC newsletter.

In 1992 Easter breakfast was organized and cooked by Linda and Jim Velvick, Gill Blackford and Mike Payne. In May 1992 Mrs Phyllis Read relinquished her position as cradle roll secretary after at least fifteen years in that post.

In July 1992 members discussed the results of a newsletter questionnaire produced by David and Rita Pocock. It was clear from the results obtained that people "wanted a replacement for The Link" rather than their own newsletter that was being produced at that time. The matter was to be pursued with Churches Together in Thatcham. By the following September Churches Together in Thatcham had agreed to produce a joint magazine bi-monthly. It was in production by January 1993. Notwithstanding that, URC members also opted to continue with the URC monthly newsletter.

THE MYSTERIOUS TIME CAPSULE

In September 1992 members had to decide whether to repair the two windows at the rear of the stage in the British School or to remove them and brick up the spaces. After discussion members voted 14-4 with 3 abstentions for the latter option. It was further agreed that a time capsule be placed behind the new brickwork, with each group within the church being invited to donate suitable items for the capsule.

In November 1992 David Pocock said "that it would be possible for a brick to be removed to accommodate the time capsule". A small time capsule was subsequently inserted in the wall between the two windows and the windows bricked up by Jim Velvick, who also repaired the stage flooring. Groups had been asked to provide items for the capsule but there appears to be nobody at the present time (2005) who can recall exactly which items were put into the time capsule.

SMOKING BANNED IN BRITISH SCHOOL

In November 1992 members agreed that smoking be banned in the British School, in the parlour and in all adjoining rooms and passageways. Appropriate notices were to be displayed. The ban came into effect on 1st February 1993.

DOOM AND GLOOM ON CHURCH FINANCES

In May 1993 the church treasurer, George Pickersgill, presented details of the financial position of the church. He said that the church had average weekly expenditure of £327 but weekly income of only £210, leaving an average weekly shortfall of £117 and a total shortfall of £2,342 for the period 1st January to 16th May 1993. The current assets of the church as at 16th May stood at £7,207, so if the level of income and expenditure continued at that level, said Mr Pickersgill, the church "would be out of funds in approximately sixty-one weeks".

In June 1993 members approved the purchase and installation of a sound amplification system for use during church services. In the following month, the applications of Allan and Ilona Crichton for church membership was approved.

Having tended her resignation from the pastorate, Revd Daphne Williams attended her last church meeting here on 20th July 1993. A farewell social and supper, with plenty of singing and stage acts, was held in the British School on Saturday 31st July - about eighty people were present on this occasion. Daphne's last church service at Thatcham URC was on Sunday 8th August 1993. She left Thatcham to take the chaplaincy of Nottingham City Hospital. In 1997 Daphne was inducted as the minister of the Church of Christ the Cornerstone in Milton Keynes. In 2001 she was appointed to the chaplaincy of the Whittington Hospital, Highgate Hill, London. Daphne married Frank Preece of Milton Keynes in 2004.

REVD NINA MEAD (1993-1998)
On 22nd September 1993 the church meeting was chaired by Revd Nina Mead as Interim Moderator. From 1988 until 1991 Nina was minister of Trinity Church, Lower Earley. She and her husband Roger then went to Dunedin, New Zealand, where Nina spent eight months as assistant minister of a Presbyterian Church in Caversham, Dunedin, while Roger was working at the University of Otago, Dunedin. They then spent three months in Australia before returning to England in 1992. Nina's next ministerial appointment was

in the team for the West Reading Group of United Reformed Churches, which she left on being appointed as Interim Moderator of Thatcham URC.

DUNSTON PARK LOCAL ECUMENICAL PROJECT

A special church meeting was held on 5th December 1993, at which the next stage of progress on the Local Ecumenical Project at Dunston Park was discussed. Some members expressed concern about the frailty of Thatcham URC's financial situation - it was generally felt that a stronger position was needed before full support could be given to the LEP. Mike Payne's proposal that Thatcham URC could not continue to support the project at that time was supported by 23-3 with 3 abstentions. St Mary's Church was to be informed.

In consequence of the foregoing decision, a special church meeting was held on 19th January 1994, when six members of the URC Reading & Oxford District Council were present. The purpose of the meeting was to consider the future ministry of Thatcham URC, including the question of whether a full-time paid minister would be appointed and Thatcham URC's recent decision on the LEP. District Council member, Colin Ferguson, pointed out that a Declaration of Intent had been signed by Thatcham URC, "which committed the whole church and therefore, the District became involved". He maintained that Thatcham URC could not withdraw from that signed declaration. Members subsequently agreed to reconsider this matter at the next church meeting on 30th January 1994. At that meeting the earlier decision was reversed. A pre-LEP Council was set up, consisting of six members of Thatcham URC and six members of the Church in St Mary's School. It was agreed to establish a Dunston Park Church, firstly at St Mary's School and later in the planned Community Hall, which opened as the Frank Hutchings Community Hall in 1997. The first church service held in that hall took place on 5th October that year.

ALAN - THE NEW SECRETARY

On 8th March 1994 Alan Mossman was appointed as church secretary, a position he has held since then to the present day in 2005. Alan took over from Doreen Pickersgill, who had occupied that post since July 1993, having been appointed on the resignation of David Weller.

NINA - THE NEW MINISTER

Following Nina's spell as Interim Moderator of the church, members invited her to become the minister and this she duly accepted on a 75% time-basis (non-stipendiary). She was inducted at Thatcham URC on 5th July 1994. Nina was born in Yorkshire, brought up in Oxford and moved to Reading in 1966. She trained as a primary school teacher and taught for about nineteen years, her last school being Fir Tree Primary School in Fir Tree Lane, Newbury, which she left in 1985 after teaching there for ten years. It was then that she embarked on her training for the church ministry and spent three years at Sarum College, Salisbury, attended by members of the Anglican, Methodist and United Reformed Churches.

Nina and Roger Mead were married in 1961. They had three children, Simon, Andrew and Rachel. Roger, who graduated from Cambridge University, moved to Reading University in 1966 to lecture in statistics. He was promoted to Deputy Vice Chancellor of Reading University in 1996. Roger retired in the year 2000. Nina and Roger currently live at Ufton Nervet, Berkshire.

NEWSLETTER - NEW EDITORS

Publication of the Churches Together newsletter (The Link), which had hitherto been edited by David and Rita Pocock, ceased at the end of 1994. Publication of the URC newsletter, produced by Gill Blackford, was taken over by Alan Mossman and Linda Velvick from December 1994.

Three of our church members died during 1994, namely Mrs Frankie Grimsley, George Pickersgill and Mrs Gladys Panting.

FAREWELL GREEN FIELDS OF DUNSTON PARK

A nostalgic walk around Dunston Park, organized by Roy Tubb on Monday 2nd January 1995, raised £13 for the George Pickersgill memorial fund. Eighteen people gathered in the British School and watched a video film produced by Trencherwood Homes Ltd, developer of about 1,100 houses in Dunston Park. The group then walked up Park Lane and along The Avenue to inspect the site of the old mansion, known as *Dunston House*, demolished around the year 1800. This was the house from which bricks were purchased by John Barfield to build our church in 1804.

A church family social for Mrs Olive Pulley was held in May 1995. Olive was soon to emigrate to New Zealand.

CHURCH CONSTITUTION AGREED

Early in 1995 members discussed and eventually agreed a constitution for the church. Salient points from the constitution include (1) A minimum of one-third of the serving elders must be present to constitute a quorum for the conduct of business. (2) Members standing for election to the eldership must receive at least 60% of those present and voting at the AGM. (3) Members must be over sixteen years of age and applications for membership must first be approved at an elders' meeting, of which there must be at least ten held each calendar year. (4) The number of serving elders is limited to a maximum of twelve. (5) New ministers are to be appointed by the church meeting with the concurrence of the URC Reading & Oxford District Council. He or she must receive 80% support of the members present and voting at a church meeting, for which written notice be given to every church member. (6) Officers of the church have to be elected annually.

During 1995 two of our members died - Mrs Lillias Franklin and Mrs Hilda Spanswick. Fred Read (husband of Phyllis Read, a constant supporter of Phyllis in her pastoral work) also died that year.

In January 1996 Mike Payne reported "two more break-ins to the (church) premises, with the loss of the new clock in the Primary Room and a handbag belonging to a Brownie leader". The police suggested that a dye be painted on window handles and that bars be fitted outside the windows. In July of that year Mike reported that another theft had taken place during the Sunday morning service on 14th July - three or four raffle prizes and sweets had been stolen. The "passageway door had not been locked".

In June 1996, when the "repair and improvement of our buildings" was under discussion, Mike Payne "expressed some reservations about the character of the building being retained if the pews were replaced by chairs".

YOUTH GUILD REUNION

On Saturday 17th May 1997, A Youth Guild reunion, organized by Janice (Chapman) Baldwin, Jackie (Rushforth) Langdon and Mary (Whitaker) Loosen, took place in the British School. Don Addicott, former leader of the Youth Guild, was present with his wife Olive. About fifty persons attended. They sat down to a meal and reminisced about the old days. As a one-off special arrangement, church members voted (March 1997) by 9-3 (with 3 abstentions) to allow low alcohol lager and a varied selection of light wines to be served at the event.

HOMOSEXUALS MAY BE MINISTERS

In July 1997 members discussed Assembly resolutions concerning the ordination of practising homosexuals. Resolution 19 declared that "no local church or pastorate is to be constrained to consider or accept such a person as its minister, nor any District Council constrained to concur with such a call". The Assembly would uphold a call to such an ordinand or minister. The Assembly would, on the other hand, uphold the refusal of a local church to call a practising homosexual as its minister. The fact of a homosexual relationship would not be permitted as a ground for rejecting a candidate for ministry in a church, assessment or entry to a college or a training course. In case of disagreements, an appeals procedure would operate. Not surprisingly perhaps, discussion on this matter at Assembly was controversial.

CHURCH RECORDS GO TO COUNTY ARCHIVES

In September 1997, following a resolution made at General Assembly to deposit significant church records into local authority depository offices - in our case Shire Hall, Shinfield Park, Reading, members asked Roy Tubb to sort all church records "with a view to seeing what can be destroyed and what should be archived at Shire Hall". This he agreed to do and in February 1998 all the important old records (including baptisms, marriages, burials, account books and church meeting minutes) were deposited at Shire Hall. A copy register of all baptisms, marriages and burials at Thatcham and Woolhampton Congregational Churches so deposited was to be kept in the church safe, together with the official receipt for all the archived documents.

On Easter Sunday 1998 Sheila Cooper, Sarah Preston, Hilary and Leroy Polhill were received into membership.

REVD NINA MEAD RETIRES

Revd Nina Mead, who had been our unpaid minister since July 1994 and before that (from September 1993) our Interim Moderator, held her last service here on Easter Sunday, 12th April 1998. Later that year Nina and her husband Roger had their church membership transferred to Trinity Church, Lower Earley, an ecumenical church, established in 1983 for the Anglican, Methodist and United Reformed Churches. A newly built Trinity Church was opened for worship at Lower Earley in 1987. Nina is currently an associate minister at Trinity Church and in 2004 she also became non-stipendiary minister for the URC-Methodist Church at Three Mile Cross, just south of Reading.

INTERIM MODERATOR AND CHAIRMAN APPOINTED

On 19th May 1998 members (only thirteen present) sanctioned the appointment of Revd Julian Macro (minister of St Andrew's URC, Reading), as Interim Moderator of Thatcham URC. It was also at this meeting that David Weller was appointed as chairman, a post he has held since then to the present time (2005).

In November 1998 Mrs Denise Cochrane gave notice of her retirement at the end of the year as our representative on the URC Reading & Oxford District Council. She had served in that post for the previous five years and had found the work, which had involved five meetings each year, very interesting. David Weller succeeded Denise as our representative on the District Council.

In March 1999 Revd Macro reported on a proposal from the District Pastoral Committee for the appointment of a full-time minister, based in Thatcham, with responsibility for Thatcham URC, Dunston Park Ecumenical Church, Theale URC and Pangbourne URC. He added that Theale URC was very weak and might close in the near future. It was noted, however, that Dunston Park Ecumenical Church was also seeking a full-time Anglican minister.

Mrs Doreen Pickersgill attended her last church meeting here in May 1999 before moving to Wootten Bassett, near Swindon, to be near her daughters Christine and Pauline and their families.

In Summer 1999 Churches Together in Thatcham agreed to buy 1,000 candles for use in the celebration of the third millennium. These were to be divided equally between the five main Thatcham Churches at a cost of £60 per church. It was suggested that each church be open for about fifteen minutes at 12 noon on 1st January 2000.

FEASIBILITY OF RENOVATION

On 28th March 2000 a special church meeting was held to consider the feasibility of renovating the church buildings. David Butler (Wessex Synod property officer and Wessex Synod Trust executive officer) was present at this meeting. A first set of drawings had been produced by Allen Associates and after discussion, members agreed to "respond positively to the feasibility study and Allen Associates be asked to prepare firm drawings of their suggestions for Thatcham URC, for approval by church meeting". An extraordinary church meeting, held on 12th April 2000, ratified the foregoing proposal 21-0 (with two abstentions). Mike Payne was elected as the project co-ordinator at this meeting.

RENOVATION PROJECT AGREED IN PRINCIPLE

On 21st February 2001 members voted to accept in principle the revised building plan by 27-3 (no abstentions). This result conformed to the minimum requirement of 75% in favour, as agreed on 23rd January last. The plan involved the construction of a new kitchen and toilets on the north side of the British School (replacing existing toilets and storeroom), widened corridor at rear and reduction in width of primary room, vestry and the parlour, several storage cupboards at rear of the stage and a disabled toilet near the old vestry. A new entrance between the British School and the church was to be added, which would lead into the sanctuary via a new doorway from the existing kitchen, the latter becoming a vestibule. Replacement of the pews by chairs was discussed but no decision was taken at this stage following strong objections from a minority of members. It was agreed to "seek further professional advice" on the matter of the pews.

In March 2001 members agreed without dissent to opt in to a new manse scheme, whereby the Wessex Synod would bring the manse up to a high standard and provide a yearly allowance of £500 for routine maintenance. Should the manse be let, then all rental income would go to the Synod. Any decision to sell a manse and buy another would need to be agreed with Synod, as at the present time.

A flower festival was held at the church over the Whitsun holiday weekend, 25th-28th May 2001, The event was organized by David and Joan Moate with assistance of "an enthusiastic group of (mainly) ladies", who clearly benefited from David's flower arranging classes prior to the event. Plants were sold and refreshments served throughout the long weekend. A sum of £2,013 was raised for the renovation project.

REVD BARBARA JANE FRANCES FLOOD-PAGE (2001-

On 27th May 2001 Revd Barbara Flood-Page 'preached with a view' at both Dunston Park Ecumenical Church and Thatcham URC. On 31st May members voted without dissent to call Barbara Flood-Page to the pastorate at Thatcham.

Barbara was born in Liverpool. When she was five years old, her parents and family moved to Birmingham, where Barbara remained until she was eighteen. Whilst there she attended King Edward VI High School at Edgbaston before proceeding to Reading University to study geography. It was there that she met John Flood-Page, an agricultural student. They were married at Exeter (where her parents were then living) in September 1964. In the following month they settled at Aberystwith, where John was doing research at the University of Wales. Barbara spent a year studying for an education diploma at the same university. In January 1966 they moved to Cannington, near Bridgwater (Somerset) and in 1970 to Garstang, Lancashire.

Barbara and John had four children, Jonathan, Patrick, Ben and Joanna. Currently they have eight grandchildren. Barbara started teaching geography in Somerset in 1968 but soon decided to spend more time with her young family so she delayed the career option. While living at Garstang, Barbara became involved with mother and toddler groups from 1971 and subsequently with her own pre-school playgroup (1974-77). It was in Lancashire that she resumed teaching geography on supply to various schools during the Autumn Term of 1977. From January 1978 until July 1980 she taught geography full-time at the Collegiate High School, Blackpool. It was then that the family moved to Lincoln, where John had been appointed as an agriculture lecturer at the Lincoln College of Agriculture. Over the next eight years, Barbara taught at secondary schools in and around Lincoln, firstly full-time geography (1980-81), then part-time (1981-82) and finally she taught various subjects on supply to local secondary schools (1982-88).

Both Barbara and John started attending the United Reformed Church at Garstang in 1972, becoming members there in 1973. Barbara began lay preaching in 1986 and was accredited as a URC lay preacher in 1989. She continued her theological training until July 1992 and was ordained as an associate minister in October that year at St Andrew's with Newland URC, Lincoln. She then worked as an ecumenical community minister in Lincoln during 1992-95 (non-stipendiary).

In September 1995 Barbara was inducted as minister of three small village churches in Northumberland - Felton, Longframlington and Glanton. It was from that pastorate that she came to Thatcham URC in 2001.

Revd Barbara Flood-Page was inducted at Thatcham URC on Saturday, 8th September 2001. By that time she and her husband John had settled in to *The (new) Manse* at 46 Foxglove Way and were busy getting to know people. (The previous *Manse*, 26 Beverley Close, was sold.) John Flood-Page had retired from his occupation as an agricultural lecturer at Lincoln in 1994.

RETURNING TO HOLLAND
In July 2001 a letter was received from Mrs Marieke Brown requesting transfer of her membership to the Reformed Church in Hoofddorp, Amsterdam, Holland. Marieke, originally from Holland, had moved with her husband Richard and family to live in Holland.

At the AGM in February 2002, church member Linda Beaumont (local district lay preacher) reported on her work during 2001. As well as leading services at Thatcham URC, she led services at Hungerford URC, Grange URC

(Reading), Twyford URC, Christchurch Woodley URC, Marlow URC and Aston Tirrold URC. Sadly, she said, she could no longer visit Pangbourne URC as that church had closed during the year. Linda preached her first full church service at Alton, Hampshire, in 1993. The following year she preached her first service at Thatcham URC. In April 2003 she transferred her membership to Dunston Park Ecumenical Church.

The funeral of Arthur Smith took place in our church on 27th March 2002. Arthur was actively involved with the Boys' Brigade in Thatcham for forty years. He died on 21st March, seventy-four years of age.

RENOVATION PROJECT AGREED IN DETAIL

At an open project committee meeting held on 10th December 2002, members considered the possibility of proceeding with the project in phases. Mr Peter Flint (URC Reading & Oxford District property officer) advised that the District be informed without delay if a phased project was desired. The project was to be divided into three phases. It took nearly two years before members were able to vote on the building plans. On 12th January 2003 they voted in excess of the required 75% in support of the proposed alterations as detailed on page 105. They also voted to replace the pews with chairs by 25-3 (those against being Graeme Panting, John Stone and Roy Tubb), to remove the existing organ and purchase a small electronic organ and to remove the pulpit completely. An open space would remain where the existing organ currently stands. In the event the organ was not to be removed - this was deemed inadmissible on historical and architectural grounds by the Listed Building Advisory Committee of the United Reformed Church.

DEATH OF WINSTON REED

Revd Winston Reed died 5th February 2003, aged ninety-five. Winston and his wife, Kathleen (née Gibbs) settled in Thatcham in 1935. They eventually took over Gibbs' clothing shop in the High Street. After war service in the Army,

Winston returned to Thatcham and very soon he and Kathleen joined the Congregational Church. In 1947 Winston was elected as a deacon and in 1948 he became the Sunday School superintendent. Shortly after that he started training as a lay preacher and in 1956 he was appointed to the Lay Pastorate of Tadley, where he served for three years. In 1959 Winston was ordained as a full-time minister at New Brunswick Congregational Church, Southmead, Bristol, where he and Kathleen stayed for five years before moving to the Congregational Church in Slough in 1964. Eight years later (1972) Winston transferred to the United Reformed Church at Marlow, his last full-time ministry. In 1980 Winston retired - he and Kathleen came to live in Newbury. Kathleen died in 1985. Winston continued to preach in local churches, including the URC, Thatcham. He married Mrs Muriel Ackworth in 1988 and moved to Wash Water. Muriel died in 1999.

MEMBERS LEARN ABOUT ISLAM

On 19th March 2003 Samina Dar, co-ordinator of the Reading Women's Muslim Association, having been invited to a church meeting, gave an interesting talk and answered questions about the Muslim faith, its similarities to and differences from the Christian faith.

COLLABORATIVE ZONING NOT WELCOMED

In July 2003 Revd Flood-Page reported a resolution from the Reading & Oxford URC District Council for a "collaborative zoning" scheme in this area. The resolution had been passed 27-10 (with 19 abstentions). This would involve Newbury, Thatcham, Hungerford, Dunston Park and Wash Water (with a total membership of about 170) being covered by just one minister. The reason for this proposal was economic - we needed to reduce the number of stipendiary ministers in the Reading & Oxford District from 18·5 to 13·5 by 2006. Not surprisingly, this resolution was not received favourably by members.

Member Ray Hutchings, husband of Stella, died 3rd November 2003, aged eighty-one. Member Isa Ferguson died 3rd January 2004, aged eighty-two.

At the church meeting on 21st January 2004, members learned that West Berkshire District Council would be determining Thatcham URC's planning proposal on 23rd February next.

RENOVATION WORK GETS UNDER WAY

On 1st November 2004 work started on phase one of the building project. This would involve the construction of a new kitchen and toilets on the north side of the British School (replacing existing toilets and storeroom), a widened corridor from the kitchen to a slightly narrower primary room (continuing to the parlour and to the sanctuary of the church), a disabled toilet on the site of the old vestry and several storage cupboards (including some at the rear of the British School stage).

Two pews (one on either side of the church) were removed in 2004-05 to provide space for wheelchair users.

BICENTENARY CELEBRATIONS

A celebration stall on the Broadway Green was organized for the Christmas Market by Thatcham URC on Friday 3rd December 2004, with banners and balloons. Mince pies and mulled wine were sold from the stall. This was the annual occasion of the big switch-on of the Christmas lights. Carol singing was accompanied by the Watership Brass Band.

A concert took place in the church on Saturday evening, 4th December. This included performances by Whitelands Primary School Choir, conducted by Karen Fakes. The Moderator, Sheila Maxey, presided at the bicentennial service on Sunday 5th December: this was followed by lunch in the British School, attended by about ninety people, including Lawrence Barfield, great-great-grandson of John Barfield, the founder of our church.

MEMORIES ARE MADE OF THIS

Several former members of the Thatcham Congregational Church were present at the bicentennial service and lunch. These included Hazel Earl (née Churchill), who wrote later that Sunday 5th December was a "real day of nostalgia" which "brought back so many happy memories of my days there - starting Sunday School at four years old, sitting on those little chairs in the church parlour, Sunday School Anniversaries, when chairs had to be put out in the aisles to accommodate everyone, then becoming a Sunday School teacher both in the morning and afternoon. Youth Guild was the highlight of the week, then followed church membership and church choir. Moving away from Thatcham, I then returned for my wedding in June 1962. So the church played a very important role in my life, for which I am very grateful."

Rosemary Stark (née Churchill) recalled that "it really was an excellent day in every way, so good to see familiar faces and places again". She added that "the church was beautifully decorated, the service was superb, the meal delicious and the atmosphere really good". She also had wonderful memories of her early life, which was centred around the Thatcham Congregational Church. One person she mentioned was Henry Robbins, organist and choirmaster. Rosemary enjoyed the Friday evening choir practices and singing in the church on Sundays. Another person remembered with affection by her was Don Addicott, who "devoted all his spare time to the Youth Guild". Rosemary joined the Youth Guild in about 1954 and "thoroughly enjoyed all the innocent fun and activities, the socials, the shows and of course the company".

Heather Moore-Scott (née Churchill) found the day "a real experience of getting strength from the past to go forward to the future". Later she recalled her memories of Miss Marjorie Brown, Sunday School superintendent and leader of the Girls' Club, who enriched Heather's early years with "her dedication and her example of service and kindness and a good Christian life". Also mentioned by Heather was Winston Reed, Sunday School superintendent and first leader of the Youth Guild. She referred to "his ability to live his faith and convey it to us without preaching it" and "his ability to listen with understanding" in her teenage years.

Janice Baldwin (née Chapman) described the 200th Anniversary Sunday as "an amazing day" with so many people working to make it a success. She later recalled her days in the Youth Guild during 1956-62. The weekly activities were "competitions, table tennis, darts, walks, dancing, lots of discussions and much friendly laughter" but one thing "stood out like a beacon" - the Annual Christmas Variety Show. The leader at that time, Don Addicott, sketched all the scenery, which was then made and painted by members. They all made costumes, learned the sketches, rehearsed the songs and sold the tickets: the show took over their lives to the extent that "most parents complained about homework not being done properly" and "too many late nights". Janice also recalled that in May 1959 the Youth Guild purchased a large canoe, the Congo Queen, which was stored at Waterside Farm close to the River Kennet. This "gave much enjoyment to those members who had passed their swimming test".

Iris Matthews was "much encouraged by the celebration of 200 years of Christian witness in Thatcham" and hoped that it would "flourish for many years to come". She first attended Thatcham Congregational Church at the age of seven with her parents and sister Olive. She went to Sunday School, then held in the afternoons. She also was a member of the Youth Guild and recalled the names of some of the shows that the Youth Guild performed, namely Showboat, Desert Song and Oklahoma - "all good fun". Iris started playing the piano for Sunday School when she was fifteen years of age and continued doing that for many years. She also played for the Youth Guild and some youth services - progressing to the organ in 1980.

Olive Hiscock (née Matthews), a former member, joined the choir as soon as she started attending the Congregational Church when she was fourteen years of age. She recently recalled that the US military forces were then based at Greenham Common and several servicemen from the base attended Sunday worship at our church and social evenings in the British School. Once a month four girls from the choir, namely Elizabeth Brown, Pamela Jones, Grace Haley and Olive Matthews, were "transported in a US military jeep to Greenham Common to lead early morning worship in the airfield chapel and then returned to Thatcham for our own service at 11 am".

Graeme Panting was impressed by the Moderator's "stirring message" at the Anniversary Service and her "examples of practical work being done in churches around the country". He later recalled that the period of ministry which most favourably impressed him was the late 1940s - early 1950s, particularly the activities of the Youth Guild under the leadership of Winston Reed. This period came under the ministries of Revds Owen and Booth. Graeme described the former as a "fiery Welsh preacher" and his wife as "a commanding, assured kind of person". Members of the Youth Guild included Winston's daughter Jane and son Graham and Revd Owen's daughters, Menna and Eryl. Graeme described Revd Booth as "a quieter man" and Mrs Booth as "a strong source of support". He recalled that Revd Roy Booth took a keen interest in cricket so it was not surprising that a Youth Guild cricket team was formed. A table tennis team was also formed and this competed in the Newbury & District Table Tennis League. During 1955-56 the Youth Guild table tennis team won the Pembroke Cup: Graeme and two of his brothers (John and Alastair) played in the team that season.

John Eggleton enjoyed a "very good anniversary weekend of events". He first attended our church during the ministry of Revd John Stay. His first memory as a young child is that of a preacher being heckled during a church service but he is not sure who the preacher was - it may have been a visiting preacher. Mrs Alice Digweed, who was Scottish, told him that heckling was fairly common in Scotland. John attended Sunday School here and remembers Miss

Hettie Peters, who 'punished' naughty children by inviting them to tea. John and two other boys had their bad behaviour corrected in that way. At least one Sunday school coach outing was to Savernake Forest. After a picnic tea in the forest the children were taken on to Silbury Hill. John recalls that he had one penny in his pocket and lost it there! That would, he said, "have bought two bags of sweets" in those days.

Until an electric organ blower was acquired in 1944, somebody was needed to pump the organ for hymns during church services and John Eggleton often performed this duty. He has never forgotten the Sunday afternoon when he flew with the Air Training Corps in a Dakota aircraft from Greenham Common to Stratford-on-Avon and was too late getting back to Thatcham to pump the organ for the evening service.

END OF THE FIRST 200 YEARS

So ends this account of the first 200 years of our church in Thatcham. Numerous events to mark the anniversary continue in 2005: these include several concerts, two plant sales, a craft and flower festival, an open garden party at the home of Basil and Eileen Pinnock, a jumble sale, a grand draw, a bric-a-brac stall on the Broadway Green, a barbecue at *The Manse* and numerous coffee mornings. It should perhaps be mentioned here that Basil Pinnock is the great-grandson of the Edmund Pinnock who became a member of our church in 1845.

Renovation building work (phase one) by Hillsdon Construction Ltd of East Challow, near Wantage, was completed in May 2005. The contract administrator and architects were Allen Associates of Bracknell. The new facilities, which cost a total of £281,193, were dedicated at a service attended by about seventy people and conducted by Revd Barbara Flood-Page on Saturday, 25th June 2005. Following the service a social gathering was held in the British School.

The Old Manse (24 Park Lane) in 1905 with Revd Jasper Frewing and his wife Maria. The youngster in the centre is probably their son Jasper. This picture appeared in Revd Summers' booklet to mark the centenary of Thatcham Congregational Church.

KEY TO PICTURES ON PAGES 118-119
a) Lawrence Barfield, great-great-grandson of John Barfield, 5th December 2004.
b) Church Flower Festival, 28th-30th May 2005
c) Anniversary Dinner in British School, 5th December 2004
d) Children from Whitelands Park School sing at the Anniversary Concert, 4th December 2004
e) Anniversary Service Day, 5th December 2004
f) Church Flower Festival, 28th-30th May 2005
g & h) Refurbishment Dedication Service, 25th June 2005

Some members of the Junior Church in 1965
Back Row (Adults): Mrs Amy Hale, Mrs Jill Wilson, Miss Susan Townsend,
Graeme Panting, ??, Miss Betty Flitter.
Front (Boys): ??, Edward Risley, John Berntsen, Anthony Amor, ??, --
Lawrence, John Walters, ??, David Eggleton, Stephen Risley, James Killbery.

Junior Church picnic at Chamberhouse Farm 1970.
Revd Frederick Spriggs is standing on the left.

Captions to these pictures can be found on page 116

The four ministers of Thatcham URC from 1974 -
Revds Nina Mead, Arthur Baker, Barbara Flood-Page and Daphne Williams.

Church elders and minister as at December 2004 -
Back Row: Alan Mossman, John Baron, Mike Payne, David Weller.
Middle Row: Joan Ball, Sandra Baron, Diane Sandell.
Front Row: Janice Baldwin, Gill Blackford, Revd Barbara Flood-Page,
Iris Matthews, Ilona Crichton.

CHURCH MEMBERS AS AT 31st DECEMBER 2004

1) Mrs Janice BALDWIN
2) Mrs Joan BALL
3) Mr John BARON
4) Mrs Sandra BARON
5) Mrs Julia BOWRY
6) Mrs Marion BROUGHTON
7) Mrs Gwen BUCKELL
8) Mr Leonard CHITSAMATANGA
9) Mrs Rhoda CHITSAMATANGA
10) Mrs Denise COCHRANE
11) Mrs Sheila COOPER
12) Mr Allan CRICHTON
13) Mrs Ilona CRICHTON
14) Mrs Grace CURTIS
15) Mrs Margaret DEMPSTER
16) Mr John EGGLETON
17) Mrs Karen FAKES
18) Mrs Mary FLETCHER
19) Mr John FLOOD-PAGE
20) Mrs Margaret GILL
21) Mrs Pauline GRESSWELL
22) Mrs Deborah GOSNEY
23) Mr Peter GOSNEY
24) Mrs Melanie GOWANS
25) Mrs Jane HEWETT
26) Mrs Christine HILTON
27) Mrs Stella HUTCHINGS
28) Mrs Esther LEWIS
29) Miss Iris MATTHEWS
30) Mr Kenny McBARNETT
31) Mr David MOATE
32) Mrs Joan MOATE
33) Mr Alan MOSSMAN
34) Mrs Gill MOSSMAN
35) Miss Eddi NEWICK
36) Mr Graeme PANTING
37) Mr Mike PAYNE
38) Mrs DOREEN PICKERSGILL
39) Mrs Eileen PINNOCK
40) Mrs Sarah PRESTON
41) Mrs Phyllis READ
42) Mrs Lee-Anne RIMPLE
43) Mr Kevin ROBERTS
44) Mrs Linda ROBERTS
45) Mrs Dianne SANDELL
46) Mrs Barbara SMITH
47) Mrs Tess SMITH
48) Mrs Rosemary SPRIGGS
49) Mr John STONE
50) Mrs Patsy STONE
51) Mrs Mary SUGDEN
52) Mr Geoffrey TODD
53) Mr Roy TUBB
54) Mr David WELLER
55) Mrs Vivienne WILDING

CHURCH OFFICERS

SECRETARIES

Stephen PINNOCK	1881-1888
William H BEBBINGTON	1888-1891
Edmund PINNOCK	1891-1895
Horatio SKILLMAN	1895-1923
Thomas Henry BROWN	1923-1931
Alfred Robert BROWN	1931-1962
Mrs L Morwen FISHER	1962-1965
Mrs Beatrice CHAPMAN	1965-1974
Mrs Amy HALE	1974-1977
Mrs Mary GRAY	1977-1980
Mrs Trudy MARDELL	1980-1982
Revd Arthur BAKER	1982-1987
Alan MOSSMAN	1987-1990
Alan COOPER	1990-1991
John BARON	1991-1992
David WELLER	1992-1993
Mrs Doreen PICKERSGILL	1993-1994
Alan MOSSMAN	1994-****

TREASURERS

John ADNAMS	-1853-1875
Thomas PINNOCK	1875-1880
John HENRY	1880-1883
Edmund PINNOCK	1883-1898
Arthur BROWN	1898-1930
A B Vincent BROWN	1930-1966
David Jeffery MARTIN	1966-1972
Mrs Janice BALDWIN	1972-1980
Mrs Ella HENSHAW	1980-1981
Mrs Janice BALDWIN	1981-1982

Mrs Joan BALL	1982-1993
George PICKSERGILL	1993-1994
John BARON	1994-1995
Allan CRICHTON	1995-****

SUNDAY SCHOOL SUPERINTENDENTS

Thomas PINNOCK	-1874-1880
Arthur BROWN	1880-1930
Miss Marjorie BROWN	1930-1948
Winston REED	1948-1955
Mrs L Morwen FISHER	1955-1959
then see below	

SUNDAY SCHOOL LEADERS
PRIMARY DEPARTMENT

Mrs Grace BENHAM	1959-1963
Miss Sue COLBOURNE	1963-1965
Mrs Rosemary SPRIGGS	1965-1973
Mrs Joyce MARSHALL	1973-1980
Miss Iris MATTHEWS	1980-1982
Mrs Barbara SMITH	1982-1995
Mrs Tess SMITH & Mrs Linda ROBERTS	1995-1999
Mrs Tess SMITH & Mrs Sheila COOPER	1999-****

JUNIOR DEPARTMENT

Mrs Hilda FLITTER	1959-1964
Mrs Amy HALE	1964-1967
Mrs Jill WILSON	1967-1977

Miss Mary LAY	1977-1982	Thomas Henry BROWN	-1906
Graeme PANTING	1982-1983	Miss Katie CARTER	1906-1917
Mrs Phyllis READ	1983-1985	Godfrey LAY	1917-1946
Alan MOSSMAN	1985-1987	Henry J ROBBINS	1946-1980
Mrs R NIMMO	1987-1988	Mrs June BAKER	1980-1989
Mrs June BAKER	1988-1989	Mrs Denise COCHRANE	1980-2002
Mrs Esther LEWIS	1989-1991	Miss Iris MATTHEWS	1980-****
Mrs Pauline GRESSWELL	1991-1995	Mrs Caroline TAYLOR	1989-1990
Mrs Gill BLACKFORD	1995-1997	Roger MEAD	1995-1998
Kevin ROBERTS	1997-2003	Wilfred LOVELESS	1995-****
Mrs Diane SANDELL	2004-****	Mrs Karen FAKES	2003-****

SENIOR DEPARTMENT

Miss Iris MATTHEWS &	
Arthur SMITH	1964-1979
Mrs June BAKER &	
Mike PAYNE	1979-1980
Mrs June BAKER	1980-1987
Mrs June BAKER &	
Mrs Esther LEWIS	1987-1989
Mrs Janice BALDWIN	1989-1990
David POCOCK	1990-1992
David POCOCK &	
Kevin ROBERTS	1992-1996
then vacant	

ORGANISTS

Mr TERRY	before July 1852-1852
Thomas PINNOCK	1852-1880
Miss WETTLAUFER	1880-
Miss Katie CARTER	1892-

CHOIRMASTERS

Miss Katie CARTER	1910-
Mr W WOODWARD	1915-
Mrs Hilda ROBBINS	1936-1936
John H MORRIS	1937-1940
Mr F WICKS	1940-1941
unknown	1941-1946
Mr C H WORSFOLD	1946-1948
John H MORRIS	1948-1951
Colin C OATES	1951-1954
Henry J ROBBINS	1954-1959
Walter BRISK	1959-1961
Henry J ROBBINS	1961-1974
Mrs June BAKER	1974-1989
then no choir	

**** current

INDEX